Common Core Writing Handbook

GRADE

5

HOUGHTON MIFFLIN HARCOURT

Contents

Contents

Writing Models and Forms

How to Use This Book

Writing is a great tool. It can help you solve problems as well as express yourself. For example, you can use it to nail down an idea or hammer out a point. This handbook will help you discover ways to use this tool well.

What Is a Handbook?

If writing is a tool, then this handbook is the how-to manual. It contains clear definitions, strategies, models, and key practice. Refer to its pages as much as you need to before, during, and after writing.

Sections of This Book

This handbook has three sections:

1 **Writing Forms**—Definitions, labels, and models of key writing forms

2 **Writing Strategies**—Ideas and methods that you can use for every kind of writing

3 **Writing Models and Forms**—Models of good writing

How to Find Information

Find information in this book in two different ways:

- **Use the contents page.** Find the section you need, and then turn to the entry that most closely matches the topic you want.
- **Use the tabs at the top of left-hand pages.** The names of the tabs change with each section. You can flip to sections that interest you to skim and scan for the information that you seek.

Purposes for Writing

Before you write, think about your purpose. Your **purpose** is your main reason for writing. The four main purposes for writing are to inform, to explain, to narrate, or to persuade.

● To Inform

To inform means share or (show information.) Informative writing gives facts and details. Some examples of writing to inform include reports, paragraphs of information, news stories, and instructions.

● To Explain

To explain means to (tell about a topic) by describing *what, why*, and *how*. You can explain a topic in any type of writing. Some examples of writing to explain are instructions, how-to paragraphs, science observation reports, and explanations.

● To Narrate

To narrate means to (tell a story,) whether that story is true or made up. Some examples of narrative writing include personal narratives, stories, and plays.

● To Persuade

To persuade means to convince someone else to agree with your opinion or to take action.) Examples of writing to persuade include opinion paragraphs, persuasive essays, and book and film reviews.

Understanding Task, Audience, and Purpose (TAP)

In addition to choosing a purpose for writing, you should consider your **audience**, or for whom you are writing. You may choose different words when writing a letter to a friend than you would in a letter to the editor of a newspaper, for example.

Once you know your purpose and audience, you can choose a **task**, or writing form. For example, if you want to share information with your class about something you've researched, you might write a report or an essay or you might make a multimedia presentation.

Before you begin writing, it is a good idea to decide your task, audience, and purpose, or **TAP**. Your teacher may give you the TAP for an assignment. Sometimes you will decide on your own.

Ask yourself these questions.

Task: <u>What</u> am I writing?

Do I want to write a letter, a poem, or something else?

Audience: For <u>whom</u> am I writing?

Am I writing for a teacher, a younger child, a friend, myself, or someone else?

Purpose: <u>Why</u> am I writing?

Am I writing to persuade someone, to give information, or for another reasons?

The Writing Process

Writing is a lot like drawing a picture. Whether you draw or write, you face the same challenge. You need to find the right form for the idea you want to express. Artists are seldom satisfied with the first sketch. More often than not, they begin to make changes almost immediately. They may add a detail here or change a color there. They may even throw away the whole first sketch. There is no one correct way to work. The only "rule" is that the finished product should be the best you can make it.

The writing process helps you move back and forth between the different stages of your writing. You can go back to any step in the process at any time.

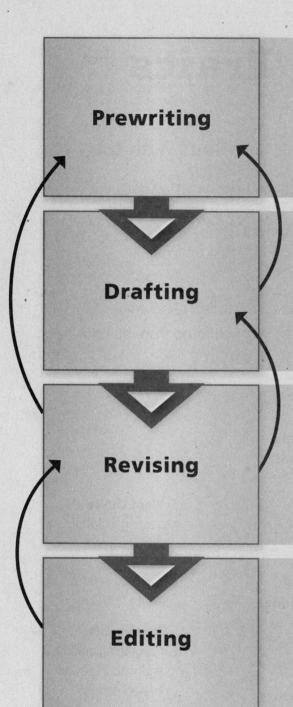

Prewriting

Identify your TAP—task, audience, and purpose. Then choose a topic. Gather and organize information about the topic.

Drafting

Put your ideas in writing. Don't worry about making mistakes. You can fix them later.

Revising

Reread your writing to see if it meets your purpose. Meet with a partner or with a group to discuss it.

Editing

Correct spelling, grammar, usage, mechanics, and capitalization errors.

Publishing

Decide how you want to publish your work. Share your writing. Examples of ways to publish include posters, bulletin boards, multimedia presentations, and oral presentations.

The Writing Traits

To cook a good meal, you have to start with the best ingredients. Likewise, to write well, you must also use the best "ingredients."

The Traits of Good Writing

The "ingredients" of good writing are six characteristics known as traits. Applying these traits to your writing will help it go from bland to exciting in no time!

Conventions
Correct punctuation, grammar, spelling

Ideas
A clear message with many specific ideas and details

Word Choice
Interesting, colorful, or exact words

The Traits of Good Writing

Voice
Clearly expressed ideas and feelings

Organization
A clear beginning, middle, and end with logically ordered details

Sentence Fluency
Sentences that begin in different ways and vary in length

Traits Checklist

As you practice writing, ask yourself these questions.

☑ **Ideas**	Did I choose a good topic? Do my ideas go with my topic? Do I have plenty of facts and examples?
☑ **Organization**	Are my details organized effectively? Does my writing have a logical order? Does the organization fit with my TAP?
☑ **Voice**	Does my voice fit my purpose? Did I include language that makes my writing interesting?
☑ **Word Choice**	Did I use clear, vivid, and interesting words?
☑ **Sentence Fluency**	Do my sentences flow together? Did I use different sentence beginnings? Did I vary my sentence length?
☑ **Conventions**	Are my spelling, grammar, capitalization, and punctuation correct?

Short Story

A **short story** is a short piece of fiction that usually focuses on a few characters and a single event.

Parts of a Short Story

- A beginning that introduces the main characters and setting
- A middle that shows how the characters react to a problem
- Dialogue between the characters
- Colorful details that describe the events in the plot
- An ending that shows a solution to the problem

Beginning
Introduces the main character and the setting

Middle
The characters react to a problem

Details that develop the plot

Ending
A solution to the problem

The students of Pod 12 were learning about the plants that grew on their home planet. Their teacher, Ms. Apple, taught them all about the different plants on Earth. Her students had never seen plants growing in the wild because they had grown up on the spaceship.

The class looked at the pictures Ms. Apple held up. "I wish we could plant a garden in our pod," said Paulo. But all of the kids in the class knew that it took years to grow plants in space.

"Maybe we can't grow our own plants, but perhaps there is another way to make a garden!" said Ms. Apple. She handed out baskets of art supplies to the class. Soon the pod was filled with giant flowers and trees.

Ms. Apple admired the pictures the students had drawn on the walls. "Your plants are so beautiful!" exclaimed Ms. Apple. "I can almost smell the flowers." Everyone in the class was smiling. They learned that there is more than one way to grow a garden in space.

Other Transitions
Suddenly
In the meantime
Afterwards
Before long
Later that day
As soon as
During

Name David K. Bland

Follow your teacher's directions to complete this page.

1 Once upon a time there was a bear cub who lived in the forest. She
refused to go to school with the other cubs and instead spent her days
fishing at the creek.

One morning while she was _getting honey from a tree minding_
her own buisness.

Suddenly, _another bear who smelled the honey came out_
demanding some honey! She responded, "I was here first."
He was furious! . Later that
morning, _while fishing at the creak the other bear went_
to her den to steal the honey.

_____. Fortunately, _she had set a trap and_
the other cub fell for it he was stuck in a net
all day.

At the end of the day, _she let him loose and they had a feast_
of fish biskets and they became good friends.

_____ lived happily ever after.

2 On a separate sheet of paper, write a short story about a
student who has to teach the class for a day.

3 On a separate sheet of paper, use your prewriting plan to write
a short story, or make a new plan to write a story about a class
that goes on an unusual field trip.

Description

A **description** uses vivid details to let the reader know how the author feels about an experience.

Parts of a Description

- An opening sentence that introduces the topic and grabs the readers' attention
- Supporting sentences that tell events in order
- Vivid words and phrases that appeal to the readers' five senses
- A closing sentence that tells what the author thinks about the events

Beginning
Attention-grabbing opening

Middle
Supporting sentences

Details that appeal to the five senses

Ending
Closing that shows the writer's attitude

I never thought I would learn to fly, but that is exactly what I did on my summer vacation. My aunt and uncle live in the Florida Keys. Last summer, my aunt taught me how to snorkel. It was the most exciting experience of my life.

We took a boat out to the reef. The reflection of the sun on the bright blue water made tiny diamonds appear on the glassy surface. When we stopped, I put on my mask and snorkel and hopped right in. The water was as warm as a bathtub. My aunt showed me how to breathe using a snorkel. I put my face under water and glided away.

Swimming over a coral reef was like flying over an alien city. Bright yellow fish darted in and out of the openings of the green and blue arms of the reef. Small red crabs raced around in the white sand below. The sea grass danced in invisible waves. Everywhere I looked there was something new to be discovered.

At the end of the day, my skin was still warm. I could still taste the salt from the ocean. I couldn't wait for my next flight through the water!

Other Descriptive Words
Shiny
Silky
Plump
Musty
Moist
Chilly
Elegant

Name David Karl Bland

Follow your teacher's directions to complete this page.

1 The one item I can never leave home without is my _phone, the_
house keys, my shoes, my socks, my backpack, my money my
shirt, my drink, and my tablet.
First of all, _I forgot all of these things excpt for my house keys_

_____

_____

_____. Sometimes, _I forget these things._

_____

_____

_____

_____

_____. Then, _____

_____

For this reason, _____

_____

_____

2 On a separate sheet of paper, write a descriptive paragraph
about what you see when you look up at the night sky.

3 On a separate sheet of paper, use your prewriting plan to
write a descriptive paragraph, or make a new plan to write a
description how you think the surface of an alien planet might
look.

Dialogue

Dialogue is the conversation between two or more characters in a story.

Parts of Dialogue

- Reveals a character's thoughts and feelings
- Sounds the way people talk to each other in real life
- Makes a story more lifelike and interesting
- Shows, rather than just tells, what is happening

> **Dialogue shows what characters think and feel**

"Quiet everyone! I now call to order the meeting of all the stuffed animals from Vivian's room!" Isaac's little sister was at it again. Her toys were spread across the living room.

"Why can't you have your little meeting in your room?" Isaac grumbled. Vivian folded her arms and glared at him.

"Isaac, why don't you try playing with your little sister instead of bugging her?" His dad didn't even look up from the paper he was reading. Isaac started to complain but sat down on the floor with a sigh instead.

> **Words sound the way people talk to each other in real life**

"Alright, Vivian. So who's the president?" Isaac asked. Vivian shrugged her shoulders. "Well, you can't have a meeting like this without a president."

Vivian looked around the room. "I know!" she yelled. "Starfox can be the president!" Their new puppy looked up excitedly at Vivian.

> **Details make the story interesting**

Isaac spent all afternoon playing with his sister. It wasn't the most fun he'd ever had, but it was better than fighting. He even smiled a little when Vivian announced, "Next, the stuffed animals go to space!"

> **Other Words to Describe Dialogue**
> Exclaimed
> Wondered
> Ordered
> Screamed
> Whispered
> Pleaded
> Sang
> Replied

Name **David K. Bland**

Follow your teacher's directions to complete this page.

1 (We Do)

It was the last day of the school year. Myra said, "_Yay! I'm so exited for summer but sadly I wont get to see you guys._

_____ "

Ms. Holiday replied, _"Ya'll can video-chat or meet up somwhere"_

At once, the whole class smiled and exclaimed, _"Six flages"_

As we left the room, Ms. Holiday said, _See you at six flages this summer_

2 (You Do)

On a separate sheet of paper, write a story with dialogue about a kid who gets to be President of the United States for a day.

3 (You Do)

On a separate sheet of paper, use your prewriting plan to write a story with dialogue, or make a plan to write a new story with dialogue about someone who makes a promise he or she cannot keep.

Fictional Narrative: Prewriting

A **fictional narrative** is a made-up story that includes a setting, characters, and plot with a problem the characters have to solve. Prewriting is the first stage of writing in which you plan your story. One way to plan a fictional narrative is to use a story map.

Parts of Prewriting for a Fictional Narrative

- Decide on an idea for your story
- Write down the names of your characters and the setting
- Think of a problem that your characters will face in your story
- Write a short description of the events that will take place in the beginning, middle, and end of your story in your story map

---

Setting: The Parkers' House

Characters: Mrs. Parker, Charlie, Evan

Plot

Beginning

Mrs. Parker thinks Charlie and Evan are eating candy before dinner.

Middle

Charlie and Evan set up a camcorder to prove someone else is taking the candy.

End

The video shows that a squirrel is stealing the candy.

Name David

Follow your teacher's directions to complete this page.

Setting School	Characters Juan, David/me, Alex, Jakai, Jeff, Cheyenne, and Joseph.

Plot

Beginning One "day" there were 7 people named Juan, Jakai, David, Jeff, Cheyenne, and Joseph. One person is the murderer. They know that. Out of all people they thought it was Jakai. They thought that because he kept on saying give me Doritos or im gonna kill you.

Middle I thought that too. He looked nice though. He is so rough. He tries to headlock me and my friends all the time. He plays too much.

End Then the murderer killed Jeff. Then Jakai got killed. He said Doritos when he died. Then they found out who was the killer. They all said its Cheyenne. So they all pressed the time bomb and everybody was alive again and Cheyenne was not a murderer again.

2 On a separate sheet of paper, draw a story map to plan a story about a group of kids who decide to form a secret club.

3 On a separate sheet of paper, make a story map for a story about friends working together to solve a problem.

Fictional Narrative

A **fictional narrative** is a made-up story about characters solving a problem, or conflict.

Parts of a Fictional Narrative

- A beginning introducing the characters, setting, and problem
- A middle that shows the personalities of the characters and the actions they take toward solving a problem
- Events told in a logical order
- Dialogue that gives each character a unique voice
- An ending that shows how the problem is solved

Beginning
Introduces characters, setting, and problem

Mrs. Parker stood in the door of her sons' bedroom. Evan and Charlie looked up from their game.

"I told you two not to eat any candy before dinner," she said with a frown. "The dish in the living room is empty."

No matter how much Evan and Charlie denied taking the candy, their mother still shook her head in disbelief.

"We'll never convince her we're innocent," said Charlie.

"We need to catch the real thief," practical Evan said, "and I know how to do it."

Middle
Tells the actions characters take toward solving the problem

First, they dug Dad's camcorder out of the closet. **Then** they hid it on the bookcase in the living room. They pointed it at the candy dish, which Mom had refilled. **Finally**, they left the camcorder running and tiptoed out.

"Now we wait for our criminal to strike," Evan said.

Dialogue
Shows what the characters are like

"This will never work," said Charlie. Charlie never thought anything would work.

Two hours **later**, they got the tape. They popped it in the VCR and hit fast forward until they saw something move. A squirrel ran out of the chimney to the dish, stuffed candy in its cheeks, and ran back.

Other Transitions
In the beginning
At first
To start with
On the first day
Second
After a while
Suddenly
At last
In the end

Ending
Tells the solution to the problem

"Got you!" said Evan. "Now Mom has to believe us!"

Name _____

Follow your teacher's directions to complete this page.

1 Jeremy yelped and shuddered as he dipped his toe in the frigid

water. _____

_____

_____. First, _____.

Then _____

_____

_____

_____

Later, _____

_____

_____

_____. To start with, _____

_____

_____. After a while, _____

_____

_____. Suddenly, _____

_____

_____

In the end, _____

 2 On a separate sheet of paper, write a fictional narrative about friends who solve a mystery.

 3 On a separate sheet of paper, use your prewriting plan to write a fictional narrative, or plan and write a fictional narrative about two friends working together to solve a problem.

Procedural Composition

A **procedural composition** explains a procedure, or step-by-step process, for doing something. It is written in time order, or sequence.

Parts of a Procedural Composition

- An introduction that tells what the essay will explain
- A body that gives the sequence of steps or events that make up the procedure
- Transition words that tell the order of the steps or events
- A conclusion that restates the topic and makes a final comment

Introduction
Tells what the reader will learn

During the California Gold Rush of 1849, many fortune hunters used a simple way of finding gold. It's called panning. Here's how it works.

First, panners picked a stream. That was the hardest part! They could never be sure where they'd find gold. Once they found a stream, they looked for a slow-moving part along a bend or near a bank. Gold is about nineteen times heavier than water, so it sinks to the bottom in slow-moving, shallow areas.

Body
Explains the sequence of steps

Next, the panners dug up about four handfuls of material from the bottom of the stream. They put it in a flat-bottomed pan with high sides. They held the pan under water and slowly moved it with a circular motion. The lighter bits of stone washed out.

Transition Words
Help readers understand the order of steps

Then the panners lifted the pan out of the water. They tipped it and swirled it until almost all the water was gone. **Finally**, they picked carefully through the remaining material in the pan. If they were lucky, they found gold.

Conclusion
Tells what the writer has learned

Can you imagine following all these steps? It took patience and practice to pan for gold. It sure was worth it, though, when someone struck it rich!

Other Transitions
Before
After that
Until
Second
Meanwhile
Lastly
The final step

Name _____

Follow your teacher's directions to complete this page.

1 We usually start each day in class the same way.

Here's what we do every morning. First, _____

_____

_____ .

Next, _____

_____

_____

Then _____

_____

_____

_____. Finally, _____

_____

_____

_____

_____

_____ .

2 Think of a chore you do at home. On a separate sheet of paper, write a procedural composition that explains how you do this chore. Explain each step clearly. Remember to use transition words to show the order of steps.

3 On a separate sheet of paper, use your prewriting plan to write a procedural composition, or plan and write a composition explaining how you get ready for bed each night.

Compare-Contrast Essay

A **compare-contrast essay** shows how two people, places, or things are alike and how they are different.

Parts of a Compare-Contrast Essay

- An introduction that tells who or what is being compared and contrasted
- A body that is organized logically: similarities first, then differences; differences, then similarities; or similarities and differences point by point
- Vivid details that make similarities and differences clear
- A conclusion that summarizes or makes a final comment

Introduction
Tells who is being compared and contrasted

Body
Lists similarities, then differences

Vivid Details
Make points clear

Conclusion
Summarizes and comments

It is hard to believe that my kittens, Wilbur and Charlotte, can look so alike but be so different.

Both kittens are light gray and have white paws. **Also**, each cat has a long, bushy tail with a bright white tip.

That is pretty much where the similarities end, however. For one thing, Charlotte loves to be out and about, and she is always getting into trouble. When I am reading, she sneaks over and tries to grab the pages as I turn them. She even got into my parents' closet and pulled down all my father's ties. She has quite an appetite, too. She is always as hungry as a wolf! She keeps following me around until I give in and put some food in her bowl. **In contrast**, Wilbur never causes trouble. He is so shy that he is always off somewhere by himself. We even found him hiding on top of the refrigerator one day! **Unlike** Charlotte, Wilbur always waits patiently to be fed.

All in all, no one would ever think that these two cats are brother and sister. Still, even though Wilbur and Charlotte are so different, everyone in our family loves them equally.

Other Transitions
Another
As well
Likewise
But
However
Finally

Name _____

Follow your teacher's directions to complete this page.

We Do
1 _____

_____

_____

_____

Both _____

_____

_____

_____

_____. Also, _____

_____

_____. In contrast, _____

_____

_____

_____

_____. Unlike _____

_____. All in all, _____

_____

_____

You Do
2 On a separate sheet of paper, plan and write a compare-
contrast essay describing two kinds of animals.

You Do
3 On a separate sheet of paper, use your prewriting plan to write
a compare-contrast essay, or make a plan and write to compare
and contrast two characters in a book you like.

Cause and Effect Essay

A **cause and effect essay** tells a cause, or reason why something happened. It also gives an effect, or an event that happened as a result.

Parts of a Cause and Effect Essay

- A topic sentence that clearly states the main idea of the essay
- A clear link between an event, or cause, and the result, or effect, of that event
- Details that support the link between cause and effect
- Transition words that help show the link
- A concluding sentence that wraps up the essay

Topic Sentence
Clearly states what the essay is about

Clear Link
Tells which event causes another

Details
Support the links between events

Concluding Sentence
Makes a comment

I forgot my lunch today because of the alien. It was just an imaginary alien, but it is still the reason I don't have my lunch.

To begin with, I was pretending to be a Martian this morning and was chasing my little brother. He loves it, and we do it all the time. He was having so much fun that he was not paying attention to where he was running. **As a result**, he tripped over our cat. The cat was frightened, **so** he ran out the back door. My little brother was upset that the cat got out, and he started to cry. **Therefore**, my mother had to stop making my lunch and calm down my little brother. **Then** she had to go find the cat.

Because she went after the cat, she forgot about my lunch. That's how I ended up with no lunch today!

From now on, I will not invade Earth until *after* school.

Other Transitions
To start with
The effect of
Since
The reason for
So that
Finally

Name _____

Follow your teacher's directions to complete this page.

1   Recycling newspapers and cardboard can help save natural resources that may run out someday. To begin with, _____

_____

_____

_____. As a result, _____

_____

_____

_____ _____

_____, so _____

_____

_____. Therefore, _____

_____

_____. Then _____

_____

_____. Because _____

_____

_____

_____

2   On a separate sheet of paper, plan and write a cause and effect essay about a small change that you can make that would have a big impact on your home or family.

3   On a separate sheet of paper, use your prewriting plan to write a cause and effect essay, or plan and write a paragraph about things that can happen because of a story.

Research Report: Prewriting

A **research report** is a nonfiction composition that uses facts gathered from several sources of information to tell about a topic. One way to plan a research report is to make an outline.

Parts of Prewriting for a Research Report

- Brainstorm ideas for your research report
- Decide on a main topic and write your thesis statement
- Research your topic and record important details on note cards
- Organize the details from your note cards into an outline that will guide you when you write your report
- Check to see that all of the details you included in your outline support your thesis

I. Introduction: The Super Bowl
    A. Exciting game
    B. Most watched sport on TV

II. History of the Super Bowl
    A. First game in 1967
    B. Originally called the AFL-NFL Championship Game
    C. Games took place in January until 2004

III. Super Bowl Records
    A. Miami Dolphins the only team to have undefeated season (Super Bowl VII)
    B. Pittsburg Steelers first team to win six Super Bowls (2009)

IV. Conclusion
    A. Winners are the best team in the world
    B. Interesting things always happen
    C. 111 million people watched the Super Bowl in 2011

Name _____

Follow your teacher's directions to complete this page.

1

I. Introduction: _____

    A. _____

    B. _____

    C. _____

II. First Settlers

    A. _____

    B. _____

    C. _____

III. Important Historical Events

    A. _____

    B. _____

    C. _____

IV. Conclusion

    A. _____

    B. _____

    C. _____

2 On a separate sheet of paper, prewrite for a research report about the history of your favorite sport or game. Create an outline to use as a guide for writing the report.

3 On a separate sheet of paper, prewrite for a research report on a science or social studies topic of your choice. Create an outline to use as a guide for writing the report.

Research Report

A **research report** is a nonfiction composition that uses facts gathered from several sources of information to tell about a topic.

Parts of a Research Report

- An introductory paragraph that tells what the report is about
- Body paragraphs with main ideas supported by facts, details, and examples gathered from different sources
- A concluding paragraph that briefly restates or summarizes the information in the report

Introductory Paragraph
Tells what the report is about

Body Paragraphs
Use facts and details to support each main idea

Information Source
Tells where paraphrased information was found

Examples
Support the main ideas

Concluding Paragraph
Summarizes the report

The Super Bowl is the championship of the National Football League. More people watch the Super Bowl on TV than any other sports event in the United States.

There are many interesting facts in Super Bowl history. The first game, in 1967, was not called the Super Bowl. It was called the AFL-NFL World Championship Game (Karlis 45). Mac Hartley's book *A Football Century* says Kansas City Chiefs owner Lamar Hunt came up with the new name. He got the idea when he saw his kids playing with what they called a "super ball." **Also**, the games used to take place in January. Since 2004, however, they have been held in February (Hazell 176).

Many records have been set at the Super Bowl. **For example**, the Miami Dolphins became the only team in NFL history to have an undefeated season when they beat the Washington Redskins in Super Bowl VII (Karlis 67). **In addition**, in February 2009, the Pittsburgh Steelers became the first team to win six Super Bowls (89).

It is not hard to see why the Super Bowl is so popular. Teams always play hard. The winners can say they are the best team in the world. Interesting things often happen, as well. Perhaps that is why 111 million people watched Super Bowl XLV in 2011!

Other Transitions
Second
Another
So
For instance
Finally
In conclusion

Name _____

Follow your teacher's directions to complete this page.

1
    Since its founding in 1559, Florida has had a rich history. Today it is still an interesting place to live. There is a lot you can learn about Florida!

_____

_____

_____. Also _____

_____

_____

_____

_____

_____. For example, _____

_____

_____

_____. In addition, _____

_____

_____

_____

_____

2
On a separate sheet of paper, write a research report about a sport you like to watch or play. Use at least two sources to find interesting facts and details to include in your report.

3
On a separate sheet of paper, use your prewriting plan to write a research report, or plan and write a new report about a social studies or science topic of your choice. Use your textbook as one source of information.

Opinion Essay

An **opinion essay** tells what the writer thinks about a topic. It also explains why the writer has this view.

Parts of an Opinion Essay

- An introduction with a clearly stated opinion
- A body with reasons to support the opinion
- Facts and examples to support the main points
- Organization that is clear and logical
- A conclusion that restates the opinion

Introduction
States the opinion

Body
Details that support the opinion

Organization
Supporting details arranged in a logical way

Conclusion
Opinion is stated in new words

Instead of having one group of students on the student council every year, there should be several rotating groups, making sure that every class is well represented. The decisions made by the student council affect everyone, so as many students as possible should participate.

Sometimes students vote for their friends or the kids who are most popular instead of voting for the students who would be best for the job. Even the kids who aren't the most popular have important ideas and opinions. Everyone should have a right to have their thoughts heard.

A lot of students don't care very much about what happens at our school. Maybe if these kids were allowed to help make decisions, they would care more about improving our school.

I think that the student council would be more effective with broader participation. Therefore, I believe that the council should be changed at least four times a year—maybe even six! This would make all the students happier and would make the school a better place.

Other Transitions
Perhaps
Additionally
Yet another reason
First of all
Also
In conclusion

Name _____

Follow your teacher's directions to complete this page.

1 I believe that our class should raise money and donate it to the _____

_____. _____

_____

First of all, _____

_____

_____

_____

Secondly, _____

_____

_____. For example, _____

_____

_____

In conclusion, _____

_____

_____

2 On a separate sheet of paper, write an opinion essay about one of the rules in your classroom.

3 On a separate sheet of paper, use your prewriting plan to write an opinion essay, or write an opinion essay on what makes a person a good role model.

Problem-Solution Composition

A **problem-solution composition** identifies a problem or situation that should be changed or fixed. Then it suggests a way to solve the problem.

Parts of a Problem-Solution Composition

- A topic sentence that clearly states the problem
- Additional sentences that explain the problem and tell how the writer thinks the problem can be solved
- Sentences offering evidence that the writer's solution is the best one and that it will work
- A concluding sentence that restates and reinforces the writer's position

Topic Sentence
States the problem

Writer's idea for a solution

Evidence and Examples
Support the writer's position

Concluding Sentence
Restates and reinforces the writer's position

We have a lot of clubs at our school. **The problem is that a lot of them are boring. Most students never bother to join them.** What's the solution? I think that a committee of students and teachers should be formed to come up with new ideas for after-school clubs.

First of all, kids know what they like. **Just as important**, teachers understand what has the most educational value. If you put the two together, you can make a great club. **For example**, how about a club that would let kids watch movies and read books? Kids would list movies that they like. Then a teacher could find good books about the same topic. Teachers could also make clubs about their subjects. Science teachers could help students form an invention club. Social studies teachers could help students set up a model government.

In conclusion, I think a group of students should meet with the school board as soon as possible to talk about setting up this committee. If teachers and students worked together, everyone would win.

Other Transitions
In the first place
Equally important
Most important
Furthermore
Additionally
To sum up

Name _____

Follow your teacher's directions to complete this page.

1 Many things could be improved in our community with help from volunteers. The problem is that students who could volunteer don't. To fix this, we should arrange special Saturdays when students can volunteer. First of all,

_____

_____

_____. For example, _____

_____

_____

_____

_____. Just as important, _____

_____

_____

_____

_____

_____

_____

In conclusion, _____

_____

_____

2 On a separate sheet of paper, plan and write a problem-solution composition about decreasing lateness among students.

3 On a separate sheet of paper, use your prewriting plan to write a problem-solution composition, or plan and write a composition about a rule you think is a problem such as *no inline skates in stores.*

Persuasive Letter

A **persuasive letter** is a type of formal letter. In it, the writer tries to convince the reader to think or act in a certain way.

Parts of a Persuasive Letter

- Business letter format, which includes a heading, inside address, salutation, body, closing, and signature
- A lead sentence that clearly states the writer's goal, or purpose, for writing the letter
- Supporting sentences that give and explain reasons for agreeing with the writer's goal
- A conclusion that restates the writer's goal

17 Palmetto St.
Palm Beach, FL 33480
July 8, 2013

William Robinson, Editor
The Summerdale Times
39 Orange Tree Rd.
Palm Beach, FL 33480

Other Closings
Yours truly
Best
Regards
Respectfully yours
Many thanks

Lead Sentence
Clearly states writer's opinion

Supporting Sentences
Give reasons and examples

Conclusion
Restates writer's goal

Dear Mr. Robinson:

I agree with your editorial that said our school should switch its yearbook from paper to online. **First of all**, students already use the Internet a lot. We go on websites all the time. It would be really easy for us to learn to use a yearbook site. **Also**, an online yearbook would be better for the earth. We would not cut down so many trees for paper. **As you can see**, our school should have an online yearbook right away. Everyone would love it, and it would help save the earth.

Sincerely,
Mary Wells

Name _____

Follow your teacher's directions to complete Frame 1.

1

_____   _____

_____   _____

_____

_____

Dear _____:

    I disagree with your recent editorial that says we cannot raise

enough money for our annual class trip to Washington, D.C. There

are a lot of things we can do. First of all, _____

_____

_____

_____

_____

_____

_____

_____

                                  Sincerely,

                                 _____

2 On a separate sheet of paper, plan and write a persuasive letter
agreeing or disagreeing with an editorial that says schools
should have art classes.

3 On a separate sheet of paper, use your prewriting plan to write
a persuasive letter, or make a new plan and respond to an
editorial that says your school needs a larger computer lab.

Persuasive Essay: Prewriting

In a **persuasive essay** the writer tries to convince the reader to act or agree with a position. Persuasive writing needs reasons to make it convincing. One way to organize your reasons is to use an idea-support map.

Parts of Prewriting for a Persuasive Essay

- Think of a clear opinion statement
- Write down the reasons to support the opinion, with the most important reason last
- Start thinking of facts and examples to support the reasons you come up with while prewriting

Title or Topic: _Starting a School Paper_

> **Opinion Statement:** Our school should start a school newspaper.

> **Supporting Reason:** A newspaper would improve our writing.

> **Supporting Reason:** A newspaper would inform students about events at the school.

> **Supporting Reason:** A newspaper could get the whole school involved.

Name _____

Follow your teacher's directions to complete this page.

1 **Title or Topic:** _____

> **Opinion Statement:**
>
> **Supporting Reason:**
>
> **Supporting Reason:**
>
> **Supporting Reason:**

 2 On a separate sheet of paper, draw an idea-support map to prewrite for a persuasive essay to convince your principal to do something to help improve your school.

 3 On a separate sheet of paper, draw an idea-support map to prewrite for a persuasive essay to convince readers to start an organization that helps the community.

Persuasive Essay

A **persuasive essay** is a composition in which the writer tries to persuade the audience to agree with his or her position or opinion.

Parts of a Persuasive Essay

- An introduction with a clear opinion statement
- A body with reasons that support the opinion, with the most important reason stated last
- Details, including facts and examples, that support the reasons
- Arguments that answer objections the audience might have
- A conclusion that restates the writer's position and may include a call to action

Introduction
Opinion statement

Body
Reasons and examples

Answer to possible objection

Conclusion
Restatement of idea and call to action

Our school has lots of organizations, including art clubs, sports teams, and academic clubs. Unfortunately, there is nothing for kids who love to write. I think we should start a school newspaper. A newspaper would help everyone.

First of all, a newspaper would improve our writing, editing, and proofreading skills. We would also learn how to interview people. **Additionally**, a newspaper could inform students about school events—and each other. **For example**, a fifth-grader just won the Science Fair. Wouldn't you love to know more about that? **Most important**, our newspaper could involve the whole school. Students and teachers could write columns, and we could even have cartoon, puzzle, and poetry contests!

You might think printing a newspaper would be expensive, but it doesn't have to be. Our newspaper could be an e-newsletter. Then we wouldn't have to pay for paper.

As you can see, a newspaper would make us better writers, report on school events, and involve the whole school. Please e-mail the principal today and help me get the first issue into your hands—or your inbox!

Other Transitions
In the first place
To begin with
Also
Specifically
In addition
Second
Consequently
Finally
In conclusion

Name _____

Follow your teacher's directions to complete this page.

1 Some students at our school aren't turning in their homework. We should start a help center. Students can sign up to get help with their studies.

First of all, _____

_____. Additionally, _____

_____.

For example, _____

_____

_____. Most importantly, _____

_____

Second, _____

_____. In addition, _____

_____. For example, _____

_____

_____. Finally, _____

_____

In conclusion, _____

_____.

2 On a separate sheet of paper, plan and write a persuasive essay to your principal about something you want to see improved at your school.

3 On a separate sheet of paper, use your prewriting plan to write a persuasive essay, or plan and write an essay to convince readers to start an organization that helps the community.

Friendly Letter

A **friendly letter** is written to someone the writer knows, such as a friend or relative. It includes informal, familiar language.

Parts of a Friendly Letter

- A heading with the writer's address and the date
- A greeting to the person who will receive the letter
- A body that makes up the main part of the letter
- An informal, friendly voice
- Interesting details to keep the reader interested
- A closing and the writer's signature

Heading
Address and date

17 Crowley Street
Tampa, FL 33609
May 5, 2013

Greeting
Greets the person receiving the letter

Dear Uncle Lou,

Body
Uses informal, friendly voice and interesting details

You'll never believe what happened! Dad and I went fishing, and I caught a huge catfish. It was really ugly. It had all these long things coming out of its face that looked like whiskers. Gross! I have never seen anything so weird. Dad said catfish were good to eat, but I didn't believe him, so I threw it back.

After fishing we went to a restaurant near the lake. There was catfish on the menu! I ordered a burger, but Dad wanted catfish. I couldn't believe he would eat something so ugly. He asked me to try some. At first, I wouldn't taste any, but then I took a tiny bite. It was pretty tasty!

You should come fishing with Dad and me sometime. If I catch a catfish, maybe this time I won't throw it back.

Your nephew,
Chris

Closing and Signature

Interjections
Wow!
Yum!
Ouch!
Hooray!
Oh!
Ugh!
Cool!

Name _____

Follow your teacher's directions to complete this page.

1

_____

_____

_____

Dear _____ ,

    I saw the coolest thing last week! _____ and I

went to _____ and _____

_____

_____

_____

_____

_____

_____

_____

                            Your friend,

                      _____

2 On a separate sheet of paper, write a friendly letter to a friend or family member about something fun you did recently.

3 On a separate sheet of paper, use your prewriting plan to write a friendly letter, or make a new plan and write a friendly letter to tell someone about a place you visited.

Character Description

A **character description** shows how someone looks, acts, and feels. It tells about the person's character, or personality.

✎ Parts of a Character Description

- Main ideas that tell about the person's character
- Examples of the person's words and actions
- Vivid details about the person's appearance and actions
- Dialogue that shows how the person talks and what the person thinks and feels

Main Ideas
Tell about the person's character

Examples
Support the main ideas

Vivid Details
Describe the person's appearance and actions

Dialogue
Shows what the person is feeling

My ten-year-old sister, Aja, is two people. Sometimes everything about her changes in an instant.

First, there's Aja the warrior princess. She's just four feet tall, but she seems taller because she stands up straight and looks everyone in the eye. Her own brown eyes are big, and when a smile lights her round face, you have to smile, too. When she's excited about something, she marches around and talks a mile a minute. For example, last week all she could talk about was the Fiery Flyer roller coaster. "I'm going to ride in the first car and not hold on!" she boasted.

Second, there's Aja the mouse, who looks like she'll scamper away any second. When we actually got to the amusement park and stood in line for the roller coaster, she stared at the huge structure. Her whole body got smaller. Her eyes grew wide, and her smile was gone. "I don't want to do this after all," she whispered, rubbing her sweaty hands on her jeans.

Aja the mouse never stays around for long, though. After a pep talk from me, she was the warrior princess again. We hopped into the second car when our turn came, held on, and had a great ride. "Can we go again?" Aja pleaded. "I'm ready for the first car!"

Character Words
shy
outgoing
silly
kind
boisterous
hard-working

Name _____

Follow your teacher's directions to complete this page.

1 _____, the main character in _____,

is an unusual person.

First, _____

_____

_____. For example, _____

_____.

Second, _____

_____

_____

_____

_____

_____

_____

_____

_____

_____.

2 Write a character description of a character from a book or a reading selection you like, or choose a public figure. Tell about two of the person's character traits. Use examples from the story or from the real person's life to support your main ideas.

3 On a separate sheet of paper, use your prewriting plan to write a character description, or plan and write a description of another fictional character or public figure.

Autobiography

An **autobiography** is a story that someone writes about his or her own life.

Parts of an Autobiography

- A beginning that tells who and what the story is about
- The pronoun *I* to show the story happened to the author
- A middle that tells the events of the story and how the author felt
- An ending that shows how the events worked out and what the author learned

Beginning
Introduces the main topic of the story

Middle
The events of the story in order

Details
Show how the author felt about the experience

Ending
Shows what the author learned

One day last year my mother picked me up from school early. I was surprised when the voice on the loudspeaker called me to the office. I didn't have a doctor's appointment, and that was the only reason I ever went home early. My mom was waiting for me. "Come on," she said. "We have to go vote."

"I'm not old enough to vote!" I said.

My mom laughed and told me that she had always enjoyed going with her mother to vote when she was little.

At the polling place, everyone whispered as if they were in a library. A woman sitting behind a long table asked my mother's name and gave her an envelope with the ballot. My mom waited her turn and then stood at a tall desk with dividers so no one could see her fill out her ballot. When she was finished, she slid her ballot into a machine. It actually was very exciting.

"Thanks for bringing me with you," I said. "I can't wait to fill out my own ballot someday!"

Other Transitions
Once
At that time
Since
Until now
As soon as
At the same time

Name _____

Follow your teacher's directions to complete this page.

1 One of the most exciting days of my life happened when _____

_____.

_____

_____

I couldn't believe it when _____

_____

_____

_____

That afternoon, _____

_____

_____

_____

_____. Then, _____

_____

_____

Later, _____

_____

_____

_____

2 On a separate sheet of paper, write an autobiography about something unusual that happened to you.

3 On a separate sheet of paper, use your prewriting plan to write an autobiography, or write an autobiography about a time when you did something that made your family proud.

Personal Narrative: Prewriting

A **personal narrative** tells a story about an important experience in the writer's life and how it made the writer feel.

Parts of Prewriting for a Personal Narrative

- Brainstorm ideas for your personal narrative
- List the important events you will describe in your narrative in a graphic organizer, such as a flow chart
- Make sure the events in your flow chart are in the correct chronological, or time, order

I got my dog Peanut right before I started third grade.

↓

He ran around and barked like a crazy little nut, so I named him Peanut.

↓

Peanut was always with me once I brought him home.

↓

I made a model of the solar system for my final science project.

↓

My dad, Peanut, and I walked to school with my model.

→

Dad tripped while carrying the model and Mars and Venus rolled out.

↓

The planets rolled under a porch where we could not reach them.

↓

I told Peanut to fetch the balls.

↓

Peanut got the model planets without breaking them.

↓

My model was saved.

Name _____

Follow your teacher's directions to complete this page.

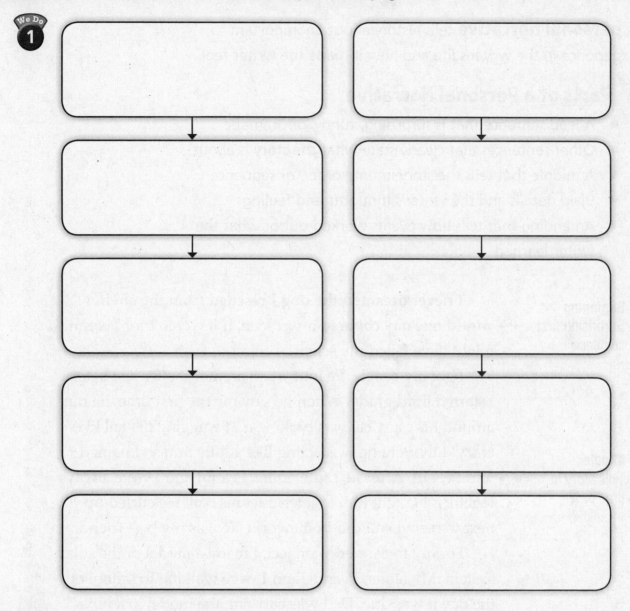

2 On a separate sheet of paper, draw a flow chart to prewrite for a personal narrative about a time a friend or family member did something to surprise you.

3 On a separate sheet of paper, draw a flow chart to prewrite for a personal narrative about a time you accomplished something you thought was impossible.

Personal Narrative

A **personal narrative** tells a story about an important experience in the writer's life and how it made the writer feel.

Parts of a Personal Narrative

- A lead sentence that is surprising, funny, or dramatic
- Other sentences that clearly state what the story is about
- A middle that tells the story in time order, or sequence
- Vivid details and the writer's thoughts and feelings
- An ending that tells how events worked out or what the writer learned

Beginning
Surprising first sentence

Middle
Tells story in time order

Vivid details and personal thoughts and feelings

Ending
Tells what the writer learned

I never dreamed the dog I rescued from the shelter would one day come to my rescue. If it weren't for Peanut, I might have failed my science project.

I got my beagle, Peanut, at an animal shelter just before I started third grade. **When** he saw me the first time, he ran around his cage. He was barking and wagging his tail like crazy! I thought he was acting like a little nut, so I named him Peanut. **After** he came home, Peanut and I were always together. I taught him to fetch a tennis ball. He curled up next to me when I did homework. He was my best friend.

For my final science project, I made a model of the solar system. My father, Peanut, and I were walking to school on the day it was due. Dad was carrying the model in a box. **Suddenly**, he tripped on a crack in the sidewalk. Venus and Mars rolled out of the box and under our neighbor's porch. Neither Dad nor I could reach the models. I could feel tears stinging my eyes. How would we save my project? **Finally**, I remembered!

"Peanut, fetch the balls," I said. He wiggled beneath the porch and brought out the model planets. He was so gentle that he didn't break either of them. I guess a dog really is a boy's best friend!

Other Transitions
First
It all started when
Next
Then
Later
As a result
That night
In the end

Name _____

Follow your teacher's directions to complete this page.

1 You'll never guess _____

_____.

When _____

_____. After _____

_____

_____. Suddenly, _____

_____

_____

The next thing that happened was _____

_____

Later, _____

_____. Then _____

_____

_____. As a result, _____

_____

_____. In the end, _____

_____

_____

2 On a separate sheet of paper, plan and write a personal narrative about a time when a friend or family member did something to surprise you.

3 On a separate sheet of paper, use your prewriting plan to write a personal narrative, or plan and write a personal narrative about a time you accomplished something you thought was impossible.

Editorial

An **editorial** is a kind of persuasive essay that appears in a periodical, such as a newspaper, magazine, or website. Some editorials respond to other articles or editorials.

Parts of an Editorial

- An introduction that states the writer's opinion or goal
- Facts and details that support the opinion
- Analogies and definitions that clarify the writer's point
- References to information sources or other texts
- A conclusion that restates the opinion

Introduction
States the writer's opinion and refers to a source

Definition

Facts and Details
Support the writer's opinion

Analogy

Conclusion
Gives a call to action

Keep the Library Open on Weekends

In a recent editorial, the *Sun Times* said, "Budget cuts are needed. Closing the public library on weekends to everyone but university students will save money and do little harm." I strongly disagree. Little money will be saved, and great harm may be done.

By definition, a *public* place is a place for everyone. Denying some people access to the public library is unfair. **In addition,** it does not cost much to keep the library open on weekends. Only four librarians are on duty, and two of them are unpaid volunteers. I also believe that cutting library hours really will harm citizens. **For example,** students without reference materials at home will be unable to work on school reports. **Also,** for busy people like me, the weekend is the only time we can read for pleasure. A weekend without books would be like a Fourth of July without fireworks!

As you can see, closing the library on weekends will do more harm than good. The city should keep it open seven days a week.

Reid Daly
Miami, FL 33299

Other Transitions
In the first place
To begin with
Additionally
As an example
In conclusion

Name _____

Follow your teacher's directions to complete this page.

1   The members of our school board have said that their biggest concern when choosing a field trip location is to pick one that will "educate and enlighten students." I think Riverside Water Park would be a perfect field trip location.

By definition, to *educate* is _____
_____
_____. In addition, _____
_____
_____

For example, _____
_____
_____
_____. Also, _____
_____
_____

As you can see, _____
_____
_____
_____

2   On a separate sheet of paper, plan and write an editorial telling whether you think your school should require all students to do volunteer work. Include a definition of a word, such as *volunteer*, to help make your point clear.

3   On a separate sheet of paper, plan and write an editorial to convince readers to start a community food bank. Include a definition of a word, such as *community*.

Response to Literature

A **response to literature** expresses an opinion about the theme, characters, plot, setting, or style of a piece of literature.

Parts of a Response to Literature

- An introduction that expresses an opinion about the text
- A summary about part or all of a story.
- A body that includes reasons that back up the opinion
- Examples from the text to support those reasons
- Details organized logically
- A conclusion that restates the writer's opinion

Introduction
Topic sentence stating the writer's opinion

→ In the short story "Off and Running" by Gary Soto, two students are running for fifth-grade class president. If I were voting in that election, I would vote for Miata. I think Miata is the best candidate.

Body
Reasons that back up the opinion

→ In the debate, Miata makes realistic campaign promises. She wants to clean up the school and make the classrooms nicer by putting flowers in them. Rudy says that he will make recess longer and have ice cream in the lunchroom every day instead of just on Fridays. These things would be more fun for the students, but it seems like Rudy is only saying these things to get votes. A student would not be able

Examples
Words and events that support the writer's reasons

→ to accomplish these changes as fifth-grade president.

Other Transitions
At the beginning
Meanwhile
Ultimately
Instead
Rather than

Conclusion
Restates the writer's opinion

→ At the end of the story, Miata's father tells her to continue her campaign even though Rudy is more popular. Miata has the best ideas of the two candidates, and I believe she would make the better fifth-grade president.

Name _____

Follow your teacher's directions to complete this page.

1 Based on the details in the biography of James Forten by Walter Dean Myers, it is easy to see that the life of the child of free Africans in 1766 was very different from the lives of children living in America now.

First of all, _____

_____.

_____

Also, _____

_____. However, _____

_____.

_____

_____

_____

_____. Most importantly, _____

_____.

Finally, _____

_____

_____.

2 On a separate sheet of paper, write a response to "The Birchbark House" by Louise Erdrich or another story you know. You might explain why you think the mother bear left Omakayas alone instead of attacking her.

3 On a separate sheet of paper, use your plan to write a response to literature, or make a new plan to respond to another story, such as "Storm Warriors" by Elisa Carbone. You might write about whether or not you think Nathan's father would have changed his mind about Nathan becoming a surfman.

Persuasive Argument

A **persuasive argument** expresses an opinion and tries to convince the reader to agree with that opinion.

Parts of a Persuasive Argument

- An introduction that clearly states the writer's opinion
- A body that gives reasons, facts, and examples to support that opinion
- Persuasive language to convince the reader
- A conclusion that summarizes the main argument

Introduction
States the main opinion, or argument

Body
Backs up the opinion with reasons, facts, and examples

Persuasive Language
Helps convince the reader

Conclusion
Sums up the opinion and reasons

Most kids today do not know where their food comes from, only that their parents bring it home from the grocery store. I think the students in our school would benefit from working in a school garden that we care for ourselves. In addition to giving us food to eat, this would also teach us valuable lessons about many different topics.

First of all, a lot of food gets wasted because so many kids take food for granted. If we were forced to work a little for the food we eat, we wouldn't be so quick to take more than we need in the lunch line. In addition, learning how to grow our own food is a skill that we could use our entire lives.

Most kids are willing to work hard if there is a reward at the end. I can't imagine anything more rewarding than eating something we grew with our own hands. A school garden would save the school money as well as provide a valuable learning experience for everyone involved.

Other Transitions
Most importantly
Likewise
Additionally
Above all
Furthermore
Consequently
In spite of

Name _____

Follow your teacher's directions to complete this page.

1   Our school is not doing enough to encourage students to become involved in the community. The student council should start a committee to help students find ways to volunteer.

First of all, _____
_____.

For instance, _____
_____
_____
_____.

In addition, _____
_____
_____
_____.

In order to _____
_____
_____ become more involved

members of our community.

2   On a separate sheet of paper, write a persuasive argument to convince your teacher to spend more time on your favorite subject.

3   On a separate sheet of paper, use your prewriting plan to write a persuasive argument, or make a new plan to write a persuasive argument to convince your readers to adopt a pet.

Response Essay: Prewriting

A **response essay** is an essay that answers a question about any aspect of a text, such as theme, plot, or characters.

✏ Parts of Prewriting for a Response Essay

- Brainstorm ideas about the story you have read
- Write down your opinion about an aspect of the story
- Using a T-map, write down reasons that support your opinion
- Write down details from the text to illustrate each reason

Topic: Greg is a smart businessperson.

Reasons	Details
He created an original product.	• His comic books were short and sturdy, not tall and floppy. • His comics could stand up on their own.
He found something he could sell without getting in trouble.	• Candy and toys were against the rules. • He realized comic books were about reading.
He put a lot of effort into making his comics.	• Greg researched how to print his comics. • He planned the comics in the series before he wrote them.

Name _____

Follow your teacher's directions to complete this page.

Reasons	Details

2 On a separate sheet of paper, draw a T-map to plan a response essay about another story, such as "Elisa's Diary" by Doris Luisa Oronoz or "Old Yeller" by Frank Gibson.

3 On a separate sheet of paper, draw a T-map to plan for a response essay based on another story, such as "Darnell Rock Reporting" by Walter Dean Myers.

Response Essay

A **response essay** is an essay that answers a question or shares an opinion about part of a text, such as theme, plot, or characters.

Parts of a Response Essay

- An introduction with a topic sentence that expresses an opinion about the text
- A body that includes reasons to support the opinion
- Specific examples from the text
- Details organized in a logical way
- A conclusion that restates the opinion in a strong, convincing way

Introduction
Topic sentence

    In the story "Lunch Money" by Andrew Clements, the main character is a student named Greg. Greg is a smart businessperson because he sells comic books at school and is very successful.

Body
Reasons to support the opinion

    Greg shows that he is smart by making a comic book that is different from other comics. Unlike comic books found in stores, Greg's comics are small, solid sixteen-page books that are easy to carry. The kids like the comics because they are unique.

Examples from the text

    Greg knew that he had to find something that he could sell in school without getting in trouble. Because candy and toys were against the rules, Greg had to think of something else. He knew that comic books would be allowed because they encourage reading.

Conclusion
Restates the opinion

    In the story, Greg was not just lucky. By making a unique product and finding a way to sell something at school without getting into trouble, he made sure he would be successful. He showed that he was a smart businessperson.

Other Transitions
First of all
Rather than
As a result
However
Incidentally

Follow your teacher's directions to complete this page.

1 In "Elisa's Diary" by Doris Luisa Oronoz, Elisa makes friends with another student named Jose. Elisa and Jose have a lot in common, but they are also different.

First of all, _____

_____

_____ .

In addition, _____

_____

_____ .

However, _____

_____

_____

_____. Instead of _____

_____ .

At the end of the story, _____

_____

_____

_____

2 On a separate sheet of paper, use your plan to write a response essay explaining why you think Elisa and her brother do not get along in "Elisa's Diary," or respond to a different story.

3 On a separate sheet of paper, use your prewriting plan to write a response essay about a story you have read, or use what you have learned to make a new plan.

Definition Paragraph

A **definition paragraph** is a paragraph that explains one object or idea in detail.

Parts of a Definition Paragraph

- An introduction that names the object or idea to be defined
- Sentences that contain facts and examples to define the main topic
- Interesting details that engage the reader
- A logical organization of supporting details
- A closing sentence that summarizes the main idea

Introduction
Names the main topic

Facts, Examples, and Details
Define the topic and interest the reader

Closing
Sums up the main topic

The monarch butterfly is one of the most recognizable butterflies. They are large insects that are easily spotted by their orange, black, and white markings. Monarchs live in both North and South America and parts of Europe, India, and the Pacific. The most remarkable thing about the monarch butterfly is how those that live in North America migrate. Every fall, millions of monarch butterflies living in cold places in the United States and Canada start flying south. Some fly as much as 2,000 miles. All of the monarchs end up in the same place in Mexico each year. The monarch butterfly only lives for two months, so no monarch butterfly makes the migration more than once. At the end of the winter, the monarch butterflies mate. The females travel north again, leaving their eggs along the way, but the males die after mating. The monarch butterfly is not the only migrating insect, but it is the most interesting.

Other Transitions
Such as
Including
Generally
Usually
In other words
Specifically

Name _____

Follow your teacher's directions to complete this page.

 1 My favorite animal is a _____.

_____

_____

These animals are interesting because _____

_____

_____

Unlike other animals, _____

_____

_____

_____

_____. For example, _____

_____

In other words, _____

_____

_____

In conclusion, _____

_____

_____

2 On a separate sheet of paper, write a definition paragraph about an animal that hibernates during the winter.

3 On a separate sheet of paper, use your prewriting plan to write a definition paragraph, or make a new plan to write a paragraph about an animal that is nocturnal, or active at night.

Journal Entry

A **journal** is a notebook in which you can write about anything you want. You can write about things that happened to you or things that you learned.

Parts of a Journal Entry

- The date at the top of the page
- A beginning that tells what the entry is about
- Interesting and important details that show your thoughts and feelings
- Don't worry too much about spelling and grammar. You are expressing thoughts and ideas for future use.

10/1/12

The Roanoke Colony is so cool! It has a really great mystery. How could a whole colony be lost? Historians still don't know what really happened at Roanoke, but our class is learning lots more about the colonies. I am really excited about our field trip to Colonial Williamsburg! Mom says I have an ancestor who lived in Virginia two hundred years ago! I want to learn more about how my ancestor lived.

Name _____

Follow your teacher's directions to complete this page.

1 Science is my favorite class. I would like to learn more about marine biology.

I'm really interested in _____

_____

_____

_____

_____

_____

_____

_____

2 I read a really great book last week. It was called _____.

It was about _____

_____

_____

_____

_____

_____

_____

_____

3 On a separate sheet of paper, write a journal entry about something interesting you learned this week.

Summary

A **summary** is a short description of the most important main ideas and details from a text.

Parts of a Summary

- An introduction that describes the main topic of the text
- A body that includes the most important main ideas and details from the text
- Transitional words and phrases to show a connection between the details and ideas in the summary

Introduction
Describes the main topic

Body
Contains the most important main ideas

Transitional Word
Shows a time relationship between details

Conclusion
Important details from the text

"Profiles of a Spacewalker" by Carole Gerber tells about the extraordinary career of astronaut Michael Lopez-Alegria. He was the commander of an expedition to the International Space Station and set the record for the most spacewalks and the most time in space in 2007.

Michael Lopez-Alegria grew up in California. As a kid, he learned about a variety of subjects. Lopez-Alegria went to the U.S. Naval Academy after high school and earned two degrees in engineering. Later, he became a Navy pilot and then started training to become an astronaut. Eventually, Lopez-Alegria helped put together the International Space Station, which he thinks was the highlight of his career.

"Profiles of a Spacewalker" gives readers an up-close look at the life of an astronaut. It also provides fascinating details about the International Space Station, which was the work of sixteen countries and which, even today, is the largest manned object in space.

Other Transitions
Before
In the meantime
As a result
At the same time
Eventually
Currently
Previously

Name _____

Follow your teacher's directions to complete this page.

1   "The Birchbark House" by Louise Erdrich tells the story of

_____

_____

After _____

_____

_____

_____

Later, _____

_____

Currently, _____

_____

_____

_____. Next, _____

_____

_____. Also, _____

_____

_____

_____

_____

2   On a separate sheet of paper, write a summary of any story in your textbook.

3   On a separate sheet of paper, use your prewriting plan to write a summary, or make a new plan to write a summary about any informational text in your textbook.

Informational Essay: Prewriting

An **informational essay** explains a topic to the reader using facts. One way to plan an informational essay is to make an outline.

Parts of Prewriting for an Informational Essay

- Brainstorm topics that you want to tell readers about
- Decide on a main topic and write a topic sentence
- Make a list of details that support the main idea
- Take the details you listed and organize them into an outline that will guide you when you write your essay

Topic Sentence: <u>The Venus flytrap is an unusual plant.</u>

I. Introduction: Venus Flytrap
   A. Found in North and South Carolina
   B. Lives in sunny and wet areas

II. Eating Habits
   A. Makes its own food using energy from the sun
   B. Also eats small insects
   C. Has leaves that trap prey
   D. Takes a week to digest

III. Conclusion
   A. Most popular meat-eating plant
   B. People take them out of the wild
   C. More in homes and nurseries than in the wild

Name _____

Follow your teacher's directions to complete this page.

We Do
1   Topic Sentence: _____.

I.   Introduction: _____

    A. _____

    B. _____

    C. _____

II.   The History of My State

    A. _____

    B. _____

    C. _____

III.   Special Events in My State

    A. _____

    B. _____

    C. _____

IV.   Conclusion

    A. _____

    B. _____

    C. _____

You Do
2   On a separate sheet of paper, plan an informational essay about an insect or plant that can be found where you live.

You Do
3   On a separate sheet of paper, plan an informational essay about a place you enjoy visiting.

Informational Essay

An **informational essay** explains a topic to the reader using facts.

✎ Parts of an Informational Essay

- An introduction paragraph that includes a topic sentence
- Body paragraphs with details that support the main idea
- Details and facts presented in a logical order
- A conclusion that sums up the essay

Introduction
Topic sentence

Body
Details to support the main idea

Logical organization of details and facts

Conclusion
Ties together the details in the essay

Many animals eat plants, but did you know that some plants eat animals? The Venus flytrap is a plant that grows in a small area in North and South Carolina. It lives in habitats that are wet and sunny, like bogs and swamps. The Venus flytrap is a very unusual plant.

Like other plants, the Venus flytrap makes its own food using energy from the sun. Unlike most plants, the Venus flytrap also eats small insects such as flies and crickets. The Venus flytrap has leaves that look like little pods. When an insect lands on one of the special leaves, the trap closes. The insect is stuck inside. It takes a Venus flytrap a week to digest one small insect.

The Venus flytrap is not the only meat-eating plant, but it is the most popular. Many people like to keep Venus flytraps as houseplants. Too many people have taken these plants out of their natural habitat. There are now many more Venus flytrap plants living in nurseries and people's homes than in the wild.

Other Transitions
Similarly
In addition
Because of
For instance
Clearly

Name _____

Follow your teacher's directions to complete this page.

1 One of the most important people in the history of my state was _____

_____. _____

_____

_____

First of all, _____

_____

_____

_____. In

fact, _____

_____

_____

As you can see, _____

_____

_____

_____

_____.Therefore, _____

_____

_____

2 On a separate sheet of paper, use your plan to write an informational essay about an insect or plant that can be found where you live, or make a new plan and write an informational essay.

3 On a separate sheet of paper, use your plan to write an informational essay about a place you enjoy visiting.

Prewriting

Writing is easier if you break the process into five stages. The stages are prewriting, drafting, revising, editing, and publishing. As you write, you can go back to any stage. **Prewriting** is the planning stage before you start to write.

Prewriting

- First, pick a topic. To brainstorm possible topics, you can make a list, look at things you have already written, or think about what has happened to you.
- Once you choose a topic, you can freewrite or make notes to come up with ideas. Circle the ideas you like most.
- Use a graphic organizer to organize your ideas and information.

❶ Brainstorm a list.

- The computer ate my homework!
- We need a computer animation class
- Computers are better than television
- Computer technology is constantly changing

❷ Freewrite

We need a computer animation class at our school. Everyone will love it. It wouldn't be very expensive. Mr. Debbs could teach it. Learning animation would be fun. It will help us get jobs one day. It could help us be more creative.

❸ Organize Information

Topic: We need a computer animation class.

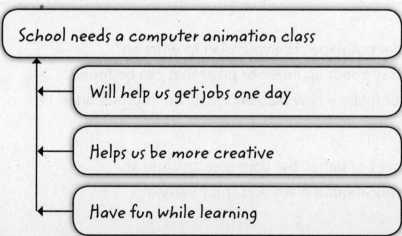

School needs a computer animation class

Will help us get jobs one day

Helps us be more creative

Have fun while learning

When you organize your information, choose the graphic organizer that works best with your Task, Audience, and Purpose (TAP).

Story Map for Narratives

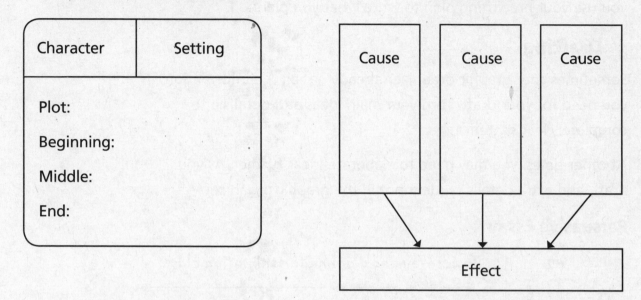

Inference Map

Venn Diagram to Compare and Contrast

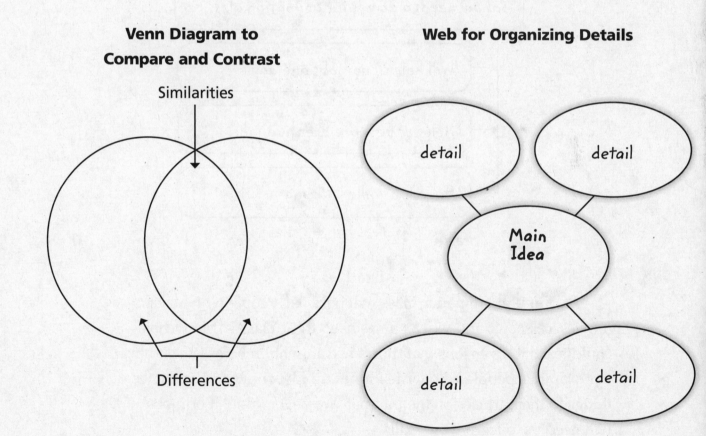

Web for Organizing Details

Drafting

Drafting is the second step of the writing process. When you draft, you use your prewriting plan to write what you planned.

✏ Drafting

Sometimes your graphic organizer already has all the information you need for your draft. Turn your main ideas and details into complete, clear sentences.

At other times, you may need to elaborate ideas further. As you draft, add extra details or ideas not in the graphic organizer.

Persuasive Essay

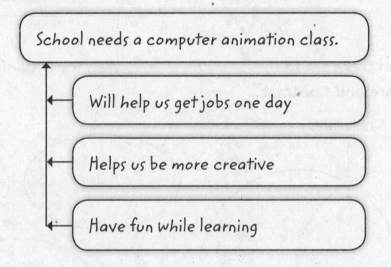

Topic: We need a computer animation class.

School needs a computer animation class.

← Will help us get jobs one day

← Helps us be more creative

← Have fun while learning

Draft

    A computer animation class will help us. People who make movies, cartoons, and video games need these classes. Mr. Debbs could teach it. Even jobs that didn't use animation before use it now. For example, people who write for newspapers now add animated things to their articles on the Internet. We never know if our jobs will need us to learn these skills.

The drafting stage is sometimes called *writing a first draft*. In this stage, put your ideas into complete sentences and add more ideas as they come to you. Don't worry if your draft is not quite right yet. You can make changes and fix mistakes at a later stage.

Fictional Narrative

Topic: "The computer ate my homework!"

teacher	Patricia
concerned, asks for homework doesn't believe Patricia	"You won't believe it: the computer ate it." She is a little afraid. tries to convince teacher

Draft

"Patricia, where is your homework?" Ms. Burns asked. She frowned slightly. "You are not usually late with it."

"You'll never believe me!" Patricia cried. "The computer ate it!" She was a little afraid of what would happen.

"Now I've heard everything," Ms. Burns said.

"It's true," said Patricia. "A big mouth appeared on the screen!"

Ms. Burns frowned. "I've never heard of anything like that before."

Revising

Revising is the third stage in the writing process. When you revise, you improve your draft.

✏ Revising

- Make sure your main ideas are clear.
- Take out information that does not support your topic or main idea. Add details that better support your topic or main ideas.
- Reorganize sentences to create a clear, logical order.
- Make sure your words and information are specific.
- Add transition words and phrases if necessary.

Ways to Revise

- Use editor's marks to show your revisions.
- Add words, sentences, or paragraphs.

Editor's Marks
≡ Make a capital.
∧ Insert.
⤺ Delete.
⊙ Make a period.
∧ Insert a comma.
/ Make lowercase.

Draft

A computer animation class will help us. People who make
get jobs one day
movies, cartoons, and video games need these classes. Mr. Debbs

could teach it. Even jobs that didn't use animation before use it now.

For example, people who write for newspapers now add animated

things to their articles on the Internet. We never know if our jobs

will need us to learn these skills. *If we take classes now,*
we will be prepared for the future.

- Cut out words or sentences you don't need.

Draft

    A computer animation class will help us. People who make *gets jobs one day* ∧ movies, cartoons, and video games need these classes. ~~Mr. Debbs could teach it.~~ Even jobs that didn't use animation before use it now. For example, people who write for newspapers now add animated things to their articles on the Internet. We never know if our jobs will need us to learn these skills. *If we take classes now, we will be prepared for the future.*

- Add information to make your writing more specific

Draft

    A computer animation class will help us. People who make *gets jobs one day* ∧ movies, cartoons, and video games need these classes. ~~Mr. Debbs could teach it.~~ Even jobs that didn't use animation before use it now. For example, people who write for newspapers now add *moving maps, charts, and pictures* ∧ ~~animated things~~ to their articles on the Internet. We never know if our jobs will need us to learn these skills. *If we take classes now, we will be prepared for the future.*

Editing

Editing is the stage of the writing process that often follows revising. During this stage, you proofread for any errors you may have made.

Editing

- Check for and correct any mistakes in punctuation, capitalization, spelling, and grammar.
- Make sure all your sentences are complete and correct. Check for run-on sentences or fragments. Also, make sure your subjects and verbs agree.
- If you edit on paper, use editor's marks.
- If you edit on the computer, use the spelling and grammar checker. Double-check your work. The computer does not catch everything.

Editor's Marks
≡ Make a capital.
∧ Insert.
ℛ Delete.
⊙ Make a period.
∧ Insert a comma.
/ Make lowercase.

Edited Draft

We Need a Computer Animation Class

in my opinion, the chance to be creativ̂e îŝ ̂are most important.

Computer animation will give us a ways̷ to learn ̷And use our imagination.

Publishing

Publishing is the final step of the writing process. When you publish, you share your writing with others.

Publishing

- When you publish, you prepare a final version of your writing to present to an audience.
- The final product can be a speech or oral presentation, a poster or visual presentation, or a printed item. You can use a computer or your best handwriting to make a final copy. You may want to include graphics, such as drawings or charts.
- You can create a portfolio of writing you want to save.

Our School Needs Computer Animation Now!

By Alexander Rothstein

A computer animation class might help us get jobs one day. People who make movies, cartoons, and video games need these classes. Even jobs that didn't use animation before use it now. For example, people who write for newspapers now add moving maps, charts, and pictures to their articles on the Internet. We don't know for certain yet if our jobs will need us to learn these skills. However, if we take classes now, we will be prepared for the future.

Ideas

Writing traits are the qualities found in all good writing. The six writing traits are **ideas**, organization, word choice, voice, sentence fluency, and conventions. Ideas are the thoughts that you will convey through your writing.

Ideas

- Brainstorm several possible topic ideas and select the one you will write about. Make sure your topic is narrow, or specific, enough to cover in one piece of writing.
- Write all your ideas about your topic in a list. Select two or three main ideas to focus on.
- Get rid of ideas that do not fit your topic.
- Organize your ideas in a graphic organizer.

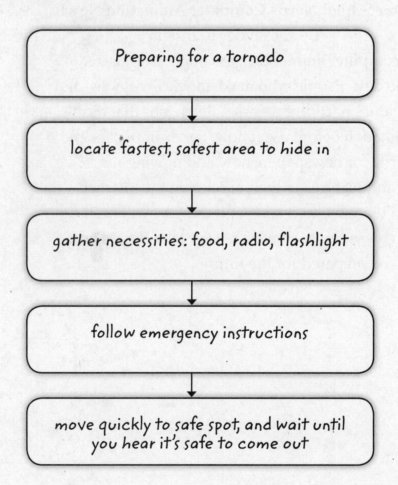

Preparing for a tornado

↓

locate fastest, safest area to hide in

↓

gather necessities: food, radio, flashlight

↓

follow emergency instructions

↓

move quickly to safe spot, and wait until you hear it's safe to come out

Narrative Writing

- Think about characters, plot, and setting.
- Good graphic organizers to use for ideas: story map, 5 Ws chart, column chart

Character	My Own Experience	Inference About Character
James likes to travel.	I enjoy taking trips. They are fun and exciting. They feel like adventures.	James is adventurous.
Sergio, James's dog, travels with James.	My dog Ralph is friendly and likes to go for walks.	Sergio is easy-going and a good companion.

Informative Writing

- Make a list of details and questions about a topic.
- Good graphic organizers to use for ideas: flow chart, note cards, KWL chart

K – What I Know	W – What I Want to Know	L – What I Have Learned
1. Scientists are studying if there could be life on Mars. 2. They send robots to gather data. The robots are called Mars Rovers.	1. What new technology are scientists using to explore Mars? 2. How can they tell if there is or was life on Mars?	1. The newest Mars Rover is called "Curiosity" 2. Scientists look for evidence that there was water on Mars.

Persuasive Writing

- Write your goal or opinion, and then think of and research reasons, facts, and examples.
- Possible graphic organizers for ideas: idea-support map, column chart, T-map

Opinion	Reasons
Hockey is the best sport.	-- It requires skill to skate and swing a hockey stick -- It's fast and fun. -- You can play outside in the winter or inside year round.

Organization

Organization is the order in which you present your ideas. Different kinds of writing need different kinds of organization.

Organization

- Choose an order of ideas that works for the type of writing you are doing. For example, a research report is often broken into paragraphs, each with a main idea and details.
- Other possible ways to organize include time order, compare and contrast, problem-solution, and cause and effect.

Narrative Writing

- Chronological, or sequential, order: the events told in the order in which they happen
- Characters, plot, setting, and a problem to be solved
- A beginning that grabs readers' interest
- A middle with interesting details about the events
- An end that tells how the story worked out or how the writer felt

Beginning →
    On my first trip to India, I was overwhelmed by the sights, sounds, and smells. It was so different from what I was used to in America. I wasn't sure I was going to like it.

    When I finally arrived at my Aunt Bina's house, I was surprised by how different her life was from mine. She
Middle →
didn't just shop at a supermarket. She went to many different market stalls for different kinds of food. It was strange, but the meals she cooked were delicious! Some of the people we saw were dressed differently than people dress at home, too. Instead of T-shirts and jeans, many women wore saris, which are long, colorful pieces of fabric they wear draped around their bodies like a dress.

End →
    It took a while to get used to, but now I love going to visit Aunt Bina! I am planning to go visit again next spring.

Informative Writing

- Information presented in a logical order
- An introduction that grabs readers' attention
- A body that presents information, explains ideas, or defines important terms
- A conclusion that summarizes the information

Introduction →

Harriet Tubman was an important person in our nation's history. Even though she could not read or write, her bravery helped save hundreds of people.

Body →

She was born a slave in Maryland in 1820. She married John Tubman, a freed slave. When she was 30, she left her family and went to Philadelphia where she learned all about the abolitionist movement and the Underground Railroad.

Conclusion →

Harriet helped to free about 300 former slaves. She bravely fought for equal rights for African Americans until she died in 1913.

Persuasive Writing

- An introduction, body, and conclusion, like in informative writing
- Reasons presented in a logical order, such as least to most important

It's good that our school's vending machines no longer sell soda. Water and juice are better options.

Reasons →

There is a lot of sugar in a can of soda. Soda might make you wake up for a while, but then you feel really tired after an hour or so. Sugar is also bad for your teeth.

A better option is juice. Juice doesn't have as much sugar, and the sugar is natural. That means your body absorbs it in a different way. Juice does not have caffeine, either. Juice has many more vitamins, too!

Voice

Your **voice** and **word choice** affect your readers. Voice is a writer's unique way of saying things.

✏ Voice

- A writer's voice lets the audience know what the writer is like.
- It sets the tone, or overall feeling, of the piece of writing. The tone shows how the writer feels about a topic.
- Match your voice with your purpose. A narrative voice should sound personal or natural. An informative voice should sound well-informed and less personal. A persuasive voice should sound convincing and positive.

Informal Voice: Use for friendly letters and personal narratives.

> Dear Penny,
>
> I can't wait to go to camp! It will be so cool to have you as a bunk mate. We'll get to do lots of hiking and boating. I'm so lucky to have my BFF going to camp with me!
>
> Love,
> Lila

Formal Voice: Use for business letters, informative writing, reports, and instructions.

> When the moon travels around the Earth, we can see the brighter parts of its surface reflected at different angles. These bright parts are commonly known as "phases" of the Moon. Each phase of the moon depends upon its position to the Sun and the Earth.

Word Choice

Good **word choice** helps paint a clear picture for readers. It helps describe characters, settings, and actions. Replace unclear words with words that are more exact.

Word Choice

- Good word choice creates a picture in the reader's mind.
- Precise words help readers know just what you mean. For example, *carrots* is a more precise, or exact, word than *food*.

First Draft

Maria and I could not get the thing to fly. Each time we tried, the wind stopped. Maria tried running one way. I tried running the other. Still, we could not get it off the ground.

"Let's try one more time," Maria said. She pointed at something.

We went up a hill. This time a strong wind lifted the kite into the sky. Maria shouted. We flew the kite until later.

Draft Revised for Word Choice

<u>My sister</u> Maria and I could not get <u>the kite</u> to fly. Each time we tried, the wind stopped. Maria tried running <u>to the left</u>. I tried running <u>to the right</u>. Still, we could not get <u>the kite</u> off the ground.

"Let's try one more time," Maria said. She pointed <u>at a hill in the distance</u>.

We <u>climbed up the</u> hill. This time a strong wind lifted the kite into the sky. Maria <u>cheered and jumped up and down</u>. We flew the kite <u>until the sun began to set</u>.

Sentence Fluency

Writing traits are the qualities found in all good writing. Checking your **sentence fluency** will help your writing flow smoothly for readers.

Sentence Fluency

- Use a mix of long and short sentences.
- Vary the way sentences begin. You don't always have to start with the subject. You can also start with transition words or phrases.
- Use a variety of sentence types, like questions, statements, and exclamations.
- Read aloud your writing to hear how it flows.

Revise choppy sentences to be smoother.

Choppy Sentences

Chantal wanted to explore caves. She needed training. Chantal knew that. But she had to take a class. The class taught her the safety rules. You needed a certificate to explore them. The park rangers would not let her do it. So Chantal took the class. She worked hard. She earned her certification. She was sure to bring a camera when she went on her first cave exploration trip.

Smooth Sentences

All her life, Chantal wanted to explore caves. She also knew she had to train and take a class on safety rules before she could do it. Without the proper certificate, the park rangers wouldn't let her explore the caves. So Chantal took the class. She worked hard and got her certification. On her first cave exploration trip, she was sure to bring a camera.

Combine choppy sentences into longer, smoother ones.

Choppy Sentences

The yard needed to be raked. The yard was covered with leaves.

A squirrel dug up the garden. He dug up carrots, lettuce, and peppers.

Longer, Smoother Sentences

The yard needed to be raked because it was covered with leaves.

A squirrel came to the garden and dug up the carrots, lettuce, and peppers.

Use a variety of sentence beginnings.

Too Many Sentences Beginning the Same Way

Sean wanted the part. Sean knew he was perfect for the role. He had practiced the lines all day. He practiced the lines while looking in the mirror. He said, "I will get this part."

Varied Beginnings

Sean wanted the part and knew he was perfect for the role. He practiced the lines all day. While practicing in the mirror, he said aloud to himself, "I will get this part!"

Use different sentence lengths and kinds of sentences.

Too Many Sentences of the Same Length and Type

Baking soda can be used for many purposes. You can mix it with water and use it to relieve insect bites. It can be used to remove scuff marks on the floor. It can also be used to clean your microwave and dishwasher.

Varied Lengths and Types

Baking soda can be used for many purposes. It can be mixed with water to relieve insect bites. Do you have scuff marks on your floor? Use baking soda to get rid of them! The next time you clean your microwave and dishwasher, adding a little baking soda can help remove odors and stains.

Conventions

Conventions are rules for grammar, spelling, punctuation, and capitalization. When you edit your writing, you check for conventions.

Conventions

- Check your writing for errors in capitalization, grammar, punctuation, and spelling.
- Make sure you begin a new paragraph for each main idea. Remember to indent the first word of each paragraph.
- Use an editing checklist and check for common errors as you edit. Use editor's marks to show your changes.

Editing Checklist

Use an editing checklist to review your writing.

Editor's Marks	
≡	Make a capital.
∧	Insert.
℘	Delete.
⊙	Make a period.
∧	Insert a comma.
/	Make lowercase.

_____ My sentences are of different lengths.

_____ I have used different kinds of sentences.

_____ My sentences are complete.

_____ I have used punctuation correctly.

_____ My words are all spelled correctly.

_____ I have used capitalization correctly.

_____ I have indented each paragraph.

Common Errors

As you write, check for common errors in capitalization, grammar, punctuation, and spelling.

Irregular Verbs

An **irregular verb** is a verb that does not end with –*ed* in the past tense.

Wrong Way	Right Way
Last night, we gived our final performance.	Last night we <u>gave</u> our final performance.
The choir singed better than ever before.	The choir <u>sang</u> better than ever before.

Commonly Confused Words

Some words are easy to mix up. Make sure you're using the correct word.

Wrong Way	Right Way
Jonny and Daniel forgot they're coats at school, so there returning their to get them.	Jonny and Daniel forgot <u>their</u> coats at school, so <u>they're</u> returning <u>there</u> to get them.
Is this you're jacket?	Is this <u>your</u> jacket?
That bread tastes well.	That bread tastes <u>good</u>.

Verb Tense

Verb tense tells us what happened in the past, present, or future.

Wrong Way	Right Way
Last week I go for a dental appointment.	Last week I <u>went</u> for a dental appointment.
I saw Jonah next Thursday.	I <u>will see</u> Jonah next Thursday.

The Verb *Be*

Be is one of the most commonly misused verbs. It takes many forms.

Wrong Way	Right Way
I is going to Jamaica on vacation.	I <u>am</u> going to Jamaica on vacation.
We was going to the beach.	We <u>were</u> going to the beach.
Tina were excited about the trip.	Tina <u>was</u> excited about the trip.

Writing Workshop

In a **writing workshop,** writers read each other's revised drafts and offer constructive criticism. Respectful comments help writers catch mistakes, correct factual errors, and improve their writing.

Peer Conferences

- Give everyone a copy of your work.
- Read aloud your writing, or have someone else read it aloud.
- When other writers read, listen attentively and take notes.
- Make specific comments and suggestions. Say exactly what you would change and why.
- Be polite and respectful. Always offer suggestions for improvement along with criticism.

Black Beauty

Author Anna Sewell wrote *Black Beauty* a long time ago. Told from his point of view, it is the story of a horse. Many good things and many bad things happen to Black Beauty. He grows up on Farmer Grey's farm where he is treeted well and has lots of friends. Then he goes to work pulling taxicabs in the big city. Mr. Nicholas Skinner is a cruel taxi owner. Finally, Black Beauty retires to the country, where three ladies take good care of him. The message of the book is to be kind to animals and to other people.

You can make different kinds of comments in a Writing Workshop.

Offer specific advice:
Instead of "a long time ago," it might be better to say the exact year.

Suggest ways to make writing better:
If you switched some words in this sentence, it would make more sense.

Help the writer with proofreading:
Double-check spelling.

Make suggestions in a positive way:
Instead of "big city," the name of the city would be a good detail.

Ask questions:
What does Skinner do that is cruel?

Offer praise as well as criticism:
Great final sentence!

Guide for a Writing Conference

The Writer's Job

- [ ] Provide a copy for each member of your group. Make notes about the writing.
- [ ] Introduce your writing. Read it aloud, or allow classmates to read it silently.
- [ ] Ask for comments and listen carefully. Try not to take the comments personally.
- [ ] Keep an open mind.
- [ ] Take notes or write down good suggestions to help you remember.
- [ ] Ask for advice about anything that caused you trouble.
- [ ] When you reread your paper after the workshop, use your notes to revise and make changes.

The Responder's Job

- [ ] Listen to or read the writing carefully.
- [ ] Make notes about the writing.
- [ ] Ask questions if you don't understand something.
- [ ] Give respectful, positive, and helpful feedback.
- [ ] Your feedback should also be specific.
- [ ] If you identify a problem in the writing, be sure to suggest a solution.

Negative/Unhelpful Responses	Positive/Helpful Responses
This story is great!	I loved the way you used rhyming words in part one. It really works.
This sounds dull.	Every paragraph begins the same. Can you change that?
Something seems to be missing.	How old is Chuck supposed to be?
This story stinks!	I think you can change a few things to make the story better.

Using the Internet

You can use your computer to research information quickly and easily.

Internet Research

- Use a reliable search engine. Enter keywords that will help you find information about your topic.

- Use websites from organizations that you know or that you can trust. Sites that end with *.org, .gov,* or *.edu* are often reliable. Try online encyclopedias, too.

- Remember to cite the sources. Include the author and title of the article or the name of the website, the name of the organization that published the website, the date the article was published, the word *Web,* and the date you accessed the information.

- If you cannot find all of the citation information, write down as much as you can.

Citation: Reynolds, Sue. "All About Snow Leopards." Big Cat Conservation Society, 6 Jan. 2012. Web. 15 Feb. 2013.

When you visit a website with useful information, be sure to write down the source.

Citation: Stevens, Patrick. "Genealogy Blog." Overlea University, Web. 26 July, 2012. patricksblog.---.com

When you use information from a website, be sure to write it in your own words.

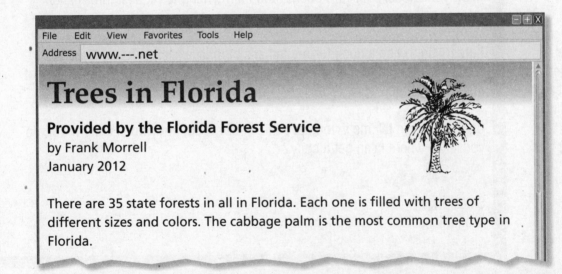

Draft

There are many kinds of trees in Florida's 35 state forests. The most common is the cabbage palm.

Source: Morrell, Frank. "Trees in Florida." Florida Department of Agriculture and Consumer Services Web. January, 2012. www.---.net

Writing for the Web

There are many ways to use technology to write. One way is to write for the web.

E-mail

An e-mail is like a letter. You can send one instantly to anyone in the world. An e-mail to a friend or family member can be informal, but an e-mail to someone you don't know well should be more formal. A formal e-mail, such as the one below, is like a business letter.

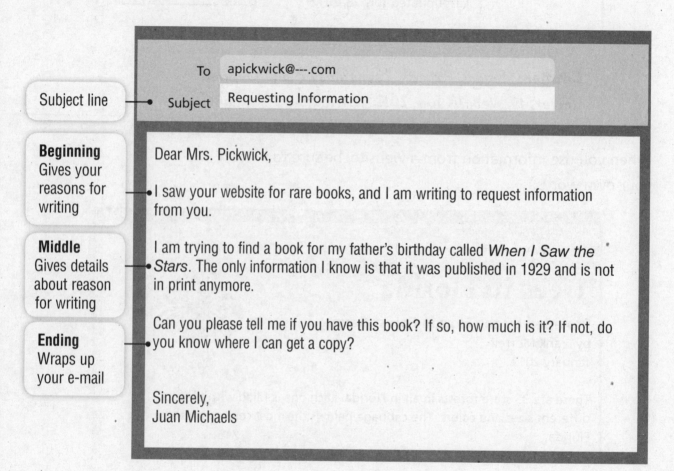

Subject line	**To** apickwick@---.com
	Subject Requesting Information

Beginning
Gives your reasons for writing

Middle
Gives details about reason for writing

Ending
Wraps up your e-mail

Dear Mrs. Pickwick,

I saw your website for rare books, and I am writing to request information from you.

I am trying to find a book for my father's birthday called *When I Saw the Stars*. The only information I know is that it was published in 1929 and is not in print anymore.

Can you please tell me if you have this book? If so, how much is it? If not, do you know where I can get a copy?

Sincerely,
Juan Michaels

✏ Blog Post

Blog is short for "weblog." It is a journal that you keep on the Internet. Other people can read and comment on it. Blog posts can be short, or they can be more like essays that give information and opinions.

URL

Blog Name

Post Title

Byline
Tells who wrote the post and when it was published

Body
Gives information, thoughts, and opinions

Comments
Left by readers

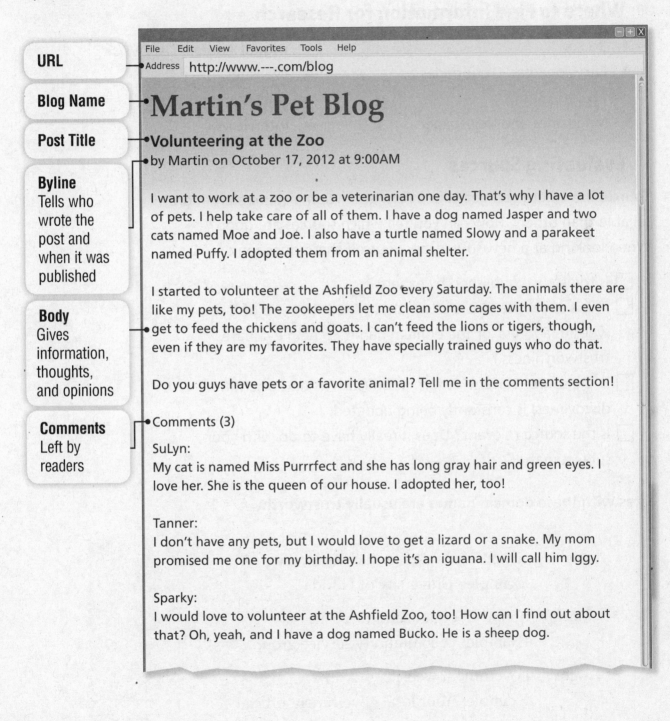

File   Edit   View   Favorites   Tools   Help

Address http://www.---.com/blog

Martin's Pet Blog

Volunteering at the Zoo

by Martin on October 17, 2012 at 9:00AM

I want to work at a zoo or be a veterinarian one day. That's why I have a lot of pets. I help take care of all of them. I have a dog named Jasper and two cats named Moe and Joe. I also have a turtle named Slowy and a parakeet named Puffy. I adopted them from an animal shelter.

I started to volunteer at the Ashfield Zoo every Saturday. The animals there are like my pets, too! The zookeepers let me clean some cages with them. I even get to feed the chickens and goats. I can't feed the lions or tigers, though, even if they are my favorites. They have specially trained guys who do that.

Do you guys have pets or a favorite animal? Tell me in the comments section!

Comments (3)

SuLyn:
My cat is named Miss Purrrfect and she has long gray hair and green eyes. I love her. She is the queen of our house. I adopted her, too!

Tanner:
I don't have any pets, but I would love to get a lizard or a snake. My mom promised me one for my birthday. I hope it's an iguana. I will call him Iggy.

Sparky:
I would love to volunteer at the Ashfield Zoo, too! How can I find out about that? Oh, yeah, and I have a dog named Bucko. He is a sheep dog.

Doing Research

The best way to support your informative or persuasive writing is to use facts and details. The best way to find facts and details is to do research.

Where to Find Information for Research

- Books
- Encyclopedias, Dictionaries, Thesauruses
- Magazines and Newspapers
- Digital Audio, CDs, DVDs
- Websites
- Television and Videos
- Interviews

Evaluating Sources

Sources are where you get your information. Some sources are more reliable than others. How can you tell which sources are good? When looking at a new source, ask yourself these questions:

☐ Is the source published by experts?

☐ If it is a website, is it trustworthy? (Check the end of the website address, or the domain name, to help evaluate trustworthiness.)

☐ Is the source current? Information (such as new scientific discoveries) is constantly being updated.

☐ Is the source relevant? Does it really have to do with your subject matter?

Sites with these domain names are usually trustworthy

> **.edu:** educational website, such as a college or university site
> Example: University of Florida
>
> **.org:** nonprofit organization website
> Example: A community service group
>
> **.gov:** government website
> Example: Your local government official

Working With Outlines

Once you finish researching, you can organize your information into an outline. To write an outline, first consider your main ideas. Then under each main idea, list the details that help explain it.

Use a Roman numeral for each main idea ➔

Use a capital letter for each detail ➔

The Three Branches of the U.S. Government

I. Legislative Branch: Congress

    A. The House of Representatives

    B. The Senate

    C. Government Agencies that support congress

II. Executive Branch: The President

    A. Head of the Executive Branch

    B. Approves bills created by Congress

    C. Official Head of the US Military

III. Judicial Branch: The Supreme Court

    A. Highest Court in the US

    B. Made up of 9 Justices

    C. Judge cases that challenge the Constitution

Outline Tips

- Choose a topic. Narrow it down so that you can be specific about your writing.
- Use only words and phrases instead of full sentences.
- Eliminate any information that will not support your ideas.
- Use your outline to help organize your ideas logically.

Notetaking

You will find a lot of information as you research. One way to keep track of it and stay organized is to take notes.

✎ Note Cards

You can put your research notes on note cards. Write a main idea or a research question at the top of the card. Then write details or the answer to your research question below. At the bottom, be sure to include your source so you don't have to go back and look for it later.

Main Idea ───▸ The Gunfight at the O.K. Corral

Details ───▸
-- The Earp brothers and Doc Holliday fought the Clantons and McLaurys at the O.K. Corral in Tombstone, AZ
-- The Earps had embarrassed Ike Clanton and Tom McLaury
-- Shots fired at close range. Tom McLaury and Billy Clanton died. Virgil & Morgan wounded, Doc was shot later. Wyatt and Ike Clanton survived.

Source ───▸ Source: Mason, Skeet. *Tales of the American West*, California: Cowboy Press, 2012. p. 144

Research Question ───▸ What really happened at the gunfight at the O.K. Corral?

Direct Quote from Source ───▸ "There is a lot of fiction surrounding the events of the gunfight that took place at the O.K. Corral. The real story was plenty dramatic."

Source ───▸ Source: Harrington, J. *The O.K. Corral, Myths and Reality*, Oklahoma: Big West Books, 2011. P. 1

Another way to take notes for a research project is to make a grid.
You can show information from more than one source.

Annie Oakley	Buffalo Bill's Wild West Show (book)	"Annie Oakley's Wild West" (magazine article)	"Annie Oakley" (Internet encyclopedia article)
Who was Annie Oakley?	exhibition shooter, performed with Buffalo Bill		born Phoebe Ann Mosley in Ohio in 1860; she began hunting at a young age
Why is she famous?	could do many tricks with a gun, toured around the US	most famous trick involved tossing a playing card in the air and shooting it	after she left the Wild West Show, she became an actress
Why did she join the Wild West Show?	started touring with circuses; joined Wild West Show with her husband Frank Butler		
What problems did she face?		many didn't take her seriously	poor family, didn't attend school
Why was she important?	first female superstar in America		set many shooting records
Other interesting facts	died in 1926 at age 66; Butler was so upset he stopped eating and died 18 days later	Famous quote: "Aim at a high mark and you shall hit it."	she also toured all over Europe

Writing to a Prompt

Sometimes you are asked to do timed writing for class exercises and for tests in different subjects, like social studies and science. This is called writing or responding to a prompt.

Responding to a Prompt

- Read the entire prompt. Make sure to follow all the directions.
- Use your time carefully and work quickly.
- First, plan your writing. Jot down ideas and details as you think of them. You don't have to use complete sentences yet. Just use words and phrases to remind you what to write.
- Use your notes to write your response. At the end, if you have time, do a quick proofread of your writing.

Sample Prompt:

Two popular forms of energy are solar energy and oil.

Which do you think is the better source of energy? Why?

Write to convince a local senator to accept your point of view.

Notes:

Solar advantages
- doesn't use resources
- clean

Solar disadvantages
- takes up lots of space

Oil advantages
- affordable
- have plenty now

Oil disadvantages
- pollution
- will run out

Solar better
- won't run out
- technology will improve

Response:

Solar power and oil each have advantages and disadvantages. Solar power is clean and doesn't use valuable resources. Oil is plentiful and affordable. But solar cells take up lots of room. Oil causes pollution and someday will run out.

In the long term, solar power is better because it won't run out as long as the sun shines. Solar cells will become smaller and more efficient in the future.

Types of Writing Prompts

There are different types of writing prompts that you may be asked to complete. Here are some of those types:

Narrative Prompt	Persuasive Prompt
Asks you to recount a personal or fictional experience or tell a story based on a real or imagined event	Asks you to convince the reader that your point of view is valid or that the reader should take a specific action
Informative Prompt	**Response to Literature**
Asks you to give information or explain why or how, to clarify a process, or to define a concept	Asks you to answer questions about something you read

Narrative Prompt:

Everyone has had a funny incident happen that they will never forget.

Think about a funny incident that has happened to you.

Now write a story describing this incident and how it happened.

Persuasive Writing Prompt:

Each U.S. president has had a unique impact on our country.

Which U.S. president do you think had the greatest effect?

Write an essay listing at least three reasons why you have chosen this president.

Informative Prompt:

Most people have at least one hobby.

Think about a hobby you have or know about.

Now write a description of your hobby and explain what materials you need.

Response to Literature Prompt:

Many people have a favorite poem or song that they like.

Think about a favorite poem or song that you like.

Now write to explain the meaning of this poem or song.

Checklists and Rubrics

Use this **rubric** to evaluate your writing. Circle a number in each
column to rate your writing. Then revise your writing to improve
your score.

	● Focus ● Support	● Organization
Score **6**	**6** My writing is focused and supported by facts or details.	**6** My writing has a clear introduction and conclusion. Ideas are clearly organized.
Score **5**	**5** My writing is mostly focused and supported by facts or details.	**5** My writing has an introduction and a conclusion. Ideas are mostly organized.
Score **4**	**4** My writing is mostly focused and supported by some facts or details.	**4** My writing has an introduction and a conclusion. Most ideas are organized.
Score **3**	**3** Some of my writing is focused and supported by some facts or details.	**3** My writing has an introduction or a conclusion but might be missing one. Some ideas are organized.
Score **2**	**2** My writing is not focused and is supported by few facts or details.	**2** My writing might not have an introduction or a conclusion. Few ideas are organized.
Score **1**	**1** My writing is not focused or supported by facts or details.	**1** My writing is missing an introduction and a conclusion. Few or no ideas are organized.

● Word Choice ● Voice	● Conventions ● Sentence Fluency
6 Ideas are linked with words, phrases, and clauses. Words are specific. My voice connects with the reader in a unique way.	**6** My writing has no errors in spelling, grammar, capitalization, or punctuation. There are a variety of sentences.
5 Most ideas are linked with words, phrases, and clauses. Words are specific. My voice connects with the reader.	**5** My writing has few errors in spelling, grammar, capitalization, or punctuation. There is some variety of sentences.
4 Some ideas are linked with words, phrases, and clauses. Some words are specific. My voice connects with the reader.	**4** My writing has some errors in spelling, grammar, capitalization, or punctuation. There is some variety of sentences.
3 Some ideas are linked with words, phrases, or clauses. Few words are specific. My voice may connect with the reader.	**3** My writing has some errors in spelling, grammar, capitalization, or punctuation. There is little variety of sentences.
2 Ideas may be linked with words, phrases, or clauses. Few words are specific. My voice may connect with the reader.	**2** My writing has many errors in spelling, grammar, capitalization, or punctuation. There is little variety of sentences. Some sentences are incomplete.
1 Ideas may not be linked with words, phrases, or clauses. No words are specific. My voice does not connect with the reader.	**1** My writing has many errors in spelling, grammar, capitalization, or punctuation. There is no variety of sentences. Sentences are incomplete.

Cause and Effect Essay

A **cause and effect essay** explains a cause, or an event that occurred. Then the author explores the effects, or what happened as a result of the event.

Parts of a Cause and Effect Essay

- An introduction that describes the subject of the essay
- Details that clearly explain a cause and its effects
- Words such as *because*, *therefore*, and *as a result*
- A conclusion that brings the essay to a close

Introduction
Tells about the subject and grabs the reader's attention

Cause: bad weather.
Effect: the class plays inside.

The word *because* suggests that the sentence includes a cause and effect.

A New Invention

One of the most popular sports of today got its start in a small Massachusetts gym over a hundred years ago. How did this sport get started?

It was December 1891, and Dr. James Naismith had a problem. He was teaching gym at a school in Massachusetts, and he needed an activity that would keep his students in shape during the cold winter months. As the weather was too bad to play outside comfortably, Naismith was forced to have class in a gym. Naismith tried to teach his students several indoor games, but they didn't enjoy the games very much. Therefore, Naismith decided he would invent something new.

Naismith quickly narrowed down the possibilities. There wasn't space in the gym for players to run very far, so his game couldn't involve too much running. Because the gym floor was hard, Naismith also knew it wouldn't make sense to let players tackle each other. Naismith decided that he wanted to develop a game that relied more on skill than on strength.

Other Transitions
As a result
Therefore
Since
So
Then
Afterward
Consequently

Cause: the school had lots of soccer balls. Effect: Naismith invented a game that used a soccer ball.

Since the school had plenty of soccer balls handy, Naismith wanted to plan a game that used a soccer ball.

On the way to class one day, Naismith asked the school's janitor if he had any boxes. The janitor told Naismith that he had two large baskets that had once held peaches and that Naismith was welcome to them. Naismith took the peach baskets to the gym and hung them from the balconies so they were a few feet above the students' heads.

Body
Explains cause and effect relationships

Next, Naismith assembled his class and explained the rules to his new game. The object of the game, he told them, was to throw the soccer ball into the peach baskets. There were 13 rules, all of which made good sense for the conditions under which the students were playing. The small space, for instance, made Naismith worry about people crashing into each other. As a result, he did not allow players to run with the ball. To move the ball, players had to pass it to a teammate.

The students enjoyed the game quite a bit. But there were a few problems. One of them involved getting the ball back after someone scored. Because the ball came to rest inside the basket, somebody had to climb a ladder and get the ball. This interrupted the flow of the game. To solve this problem, Naismith cut out the bottoms of the baskets. Now, when the ball went into a basket, it fell out the other end and the game could keep going.

Conclusion
Wraps up the essay

Word soon spread to other schools about Naismith's new game. Because Naismith's new game was good fun and good exercise, it became more and more popular. Today it's as popular as ever. What is it? Well, as you've no doubt figured out, Naismith's invention was basketball!

Problem-Solution Composition

A **problem-solution composition** describes a specific problem, or conflict, and then explores possible solutions to the problem.

Parts of a Problem-Solution Composition

- An opening paragraph that introduces the problem
- Specific examples to help define the problem
- A paragraph that explores possible solutions
- A conclusion to tie the ideas together

Introduction
Explains the topic by introducing the problem

Too Many Deer!

Throughout much of the Northeast, there are too many deer running wild. Although deer are beautiful animals, too many deer can lead to serious problems with humans and the environment. These problems affect everything from roads to forests.

Hundreds of years ago, there were not as many people living in the Northeast. At the same time, there were many wolves, bears, and coyotes. These large predators helped keep the deer population in check by removing unhealthy or weak deer from herds. Over time, humans hunted more of these large predators, and very few are left today. Without natural predators, the deer populations exploded across the Northeast.

Other Transitions
Although
In addition
Over time
Worse yet
Another
Unfortunately
Fortunately

Deer move around a lot. This causes major problems for motorists. Even though signs along major highways in the Northeast warn drivers to watch out for deer, cars still hit deer as the animals try to cross the road. Hitting deer can cause serious damage to people's cars. Worse yet, these accidents can be deadly for humans and deer.

Body
Gives details and examples to explain the problem

The author continues to expand on the problem by providing more examples.

Also, having too many deer can hurt forests and home gardens. Slow-growing trees like oak, ash, and maple grow all over the Northeast. Unfortunately, the leaves of young trees are a favorite food for deer. When deer enter a forest, they eat all the leaves before the young trees have a chance to grow big and strong. Without young trees replacing old ones, a forest will slowly die off.

Fortunately, there are many solutions to the deer problem. Mowing along roadways to cut down tall grass can reduce car crashes caused by deer. Drivers will be able to see deer before the animals wander into the road. This can save the lives of humans and deer. A possible solution to help save forests is to build tall fences around parts of the forests. These fences would keep out the deer. Then the young trees can keep growing and our forests can stay healthy. Everyone can help to put up these fences.

Conclusion
Offers possible solutions and wraps up the essay

Solving the deer problem will take time. But it is worth it to make sure that animals and humans stay safe and happy.

Note how the author of this essay:

- Began the essay by introducing the problem.

  Another way the author could have begun the essay is to paint a picture to grab the reader's attention.

  Sometimes it can be fun to see wild animals. Deer run fast and hide, so you don't often see them. Unfortunately, in some places, there are too many deer.

- Gave background information to explain the problem.

  Hundreds of years ago, there were not as many people living in the Northeast.

Compare and Contrast Essay

A **compare and contrast essay** is a form of writing that examines the similarities and differences between two people, places, or things.

Parts of a Compare and Contrast Essay

- An introduction to the subjects being compared
- A body that clearly shows similarities and differences point by point; each paragraph should focus on one specific topic
- Details and facts that identify the similarities and differences
- A conclusion that reviews the main points of the essay

The Greatest Ever?

Wilt Chamberlain vs. Michael Jordan

Introduction
Tells about the subject and the main topics that the essay will address

Who is the greatest basketball player to ever play the game? Two candidates for that title are Wilt Chamberlain and Michael Jordan. Both players were famous during the time they played, and both players broke many records. At the same time, both players also had very different styles that led to their success.

Facts and details support the main ideas.

Wilt Chamberlain and Michael Jordan were both college stars. Wilt Chamberlain played center at the University of Kansas from 1955 to 1958. Even though Chamberlain played very well in college, he was never able to win a national college championship. Michael Jordan attended the University of North Carolina, where he played the guard position. Unlike Chamberlain, Jordan won a college championship. In 1982, he made the winning shot that helped his team beat the Georgetown Hoyas and win the national title.

Both Chamberlain and Jordan left college early to play professional basketball. Chamberlain went on to star with the

Other Transitions
At the same time
Meanwhile
Although
On the other hand

Details show
similarities.

Philadelphia 76ers and Los Angeles Lakers in the National
Basketball Association (NBA). In his first year, Chamberlain
was named the league's Most Valuable Player and Rookie of
the Year. Jordan did well in the NBA too. He was picked up
by the Chicago Bulls in 1984 and was also named Rookie of
the Year during his first professional season. Both players
had very successful professional careers. Chamberlain led
his teams to four NBA championships. Meanwhile, Jordan
went on to win six championships. Both players are honored
in the NBA Hall of Fame.

Details show
differences.

Although both players excelled in their day, Wilt
Chamberlain and Michael Jordan had two very different
styles of play. Chamberlain was more than seven feet tall
and played center. Because he was so tall, he could easily
score points. In one NBA game in 1962, he scored an
amazing 100 points, a record that still stands to this day!
Jordan, on the other hand, was a fast and agile shooting
guard. He was graceful to watch and could soar through the
air to make incredible dunks.

Conclusion
Reviews
the main
similarities and
differences
and draws a
conclusion

Both players can be recognized for changing the game
of basketball. Wilt Chamberlain was a dominant center who
could score points and block shots almost at will. Having a
dominant center that could play both offense and defense
would become an important part of a successful basketball
team in the NBA. Jordan, on the other hand, changed the
modern game. He was exciting to watch almost every time
he got the ball. He could dazzle players with his moves and
soar through the air to make amazing shots. Like
Chamberlain, Jordan excelled at both offense and defense.
Both players contributed greatly to professional basketball.
Although they played two different positions in very
different eras, both can be considered the best to ever have
picked up a basketball.

How-to Essay

A **how-to essay** describes how to do something that the reader may not be familiar with. This type of essay has very clear step-by-step directions to help the reader complete the project.

Parts of a How-to Essay

- An introduction that gets the reader interested in the project
- Paragraphs that clearly explain how the reader can complete the project
- A conclusion that reviews some of the essay's basic concepts

Beginning
Uses engaging language to introduce the project

Details tell what you need to get started.

Steps are described in order.

How to Start Beekeeping

Beekeeping can be a fun and rewarding hobby for all ages. Not only are you giving bees a place to live, but you also get to enjoy the rewards of this wonderful hobby. One beehive can produce gallons of delicious homemade honey each year. The best thing is, it is easy to get started!

The first thing you will want to do is to get an adult to help you. Then, check with your family and neighbors about your new hobby. Bees can be dangerous when they sting, and some people won't like this. Also, learn about local laws about beekeeping. Some towns and cities do not allow beekeeping.

Your next step is choosing the right place to put your hive. If you have a small yard, you will probably only want one or two hives. A corner far away from your house is a good place to set up a hive for your bees. This way the bees won't bother your family or pets, and they will have a safe place to live.

After you find a good place for a hive, choose which kind of beehive you want. One good choice is a moveable frame hive. It has lots of places for the bees to build their honeycomb and produce a lot of honey.

Other transitions
Not only
The first thing
Also
Your next step
Therefore
However
Once
Next
Finally

Each step of the project is supported with reasons as to why these steps are important.

Once you have chosen the type of hive you want, make sure you have all the other necessary equipment. A full protective suit with hat, veil, and gloves is a must to protect yourself from stings. A smoker is also valuable in order to calm the bees when you extract honey. You will also want a scraping tool to remove all that wonderful honey!

Finally, figure out where you are going to get your bees. Use the Internet to research places that sell bees. Most places can mail you a box of bees that will help you get started. But make sure you do your research! Certain types of bees are adapted to different climates. Make sure the bees you purchase can survive in the climate you live in.

Beekeeping is getting more popular every year. There are plenty of resources in books and on the Internet to help you get started with your new hobby. If it's done well, beekeeping can be a fun and educational experience for the whole family to enjoy. And just think of all that honey!

Conclusion Reviews some of the main points to the essay and reminds the readers why they might be interested

Note how the author of this piece:

- Started the essay with reasons why the reader should complete the project.

  One beehive can produce gallons of delicious homemade honey each year. The best thing is, it is easy to get started!

- Clearly stated a main idea in each paragraph and offered details that would support that main idea.

- Offered ideas to continue exploring this subject in the library or on the Internet.

Explanation

An **explanation essay** is used to describe or inform about a subject. This type of essay is well researched and organized to present information clearly.

Parts of an Explanation Essay

- An introduction that describes what the essay is about and why
- Body paragraphs with facts and details that support the main idea
- A conclusion that summarizes the essay's main idea

Introduction
Explains the topic of the essay and tells the main idea

Animal Hibernation

All animals have developed ways to adapt when food is hard to find. Some animals have learned to hide food and save it for the winter. Many species of birds and fish migrate to warmer climates where there is much more food. However, other animals just can't move as far to escape the cold winter. Instead, these animals sleep through the winter months. Hibernation allows animals to survive when there is less food.

Animals burn a lot of energy every day. Warm-blooded animals, such as mammals, need a lot of energy just to keep up their body temperature. So, you can imagine that running, flying, climbing, and doing other animal activities takes even more energy. Animals get energy from the food they eat. When animals hibernate, they need very little energy. A hibernating animal's breathing and heart rate slow down, and its body temperature drops. As a result, the animal uses less energy and needs less food. This allows an animal to survive a long winter by simply sleeping through it!

Some mammals, such as bears and bats, hibernate through the winter. Ever see a plump chipmunk busily

Transition words
However
Instead
So
Such as
Too
Even so

Body
Uses researched facts and details to support the main idea

collecting acorns during autumn? There's a good reason for this. Chipmunks, bears, and other hibernating mammals eat more food than normal right before hibernation. This extra food is stored in fat cells that can then be burned during hibernation and used as energy. The fatter the chipmunk, the better chance it has of surviving a long, cold winter without food.

The author expands on the subject by giving examples of different kinds of hibernation.

Even some reptiles and amphibians hibernate, too. Unlike mammals, these animals are cold-blooded and rely on the sun and warm air to maintain body temperature. Amphibians, such as frogs, hibernate by burying themselves in mud or resting at the bottom of ponds. Reptiles, such as snakes, hibernate deep in the ground in holes dug by other animals. They go so far into the ground that cold air can't harm them.

Conclusion Reviews the essay's main ideas

The animal kingdom has many stories to tell. All animals have to adapt to changing conditions. If they don't, they won't survive. Hibernation is one amazing way animals have learned to adapt to difficult conditions.

Note how the author of this piece:

- Used transitions to explain how hibernation helps animals survive.

  A hibernating animal's breathing and heart rate slow down, and its body temperature drops. **As a result,** the animal uses less energy and needs less food.

- Used examples from readers' experiences to make the explanation more understandable.

  Ever see a plump chipmunk busily collecting acorns during autumn?

Definition Essay

A **definition essay** explains something in detail. It focuses on one thing or idea and tells what it means, what it is, or what it does.

Parts of a Definition Essay

- An introduction that tells what is to be defined
- A body that uses interesting facts and details to support the main idea
- A conclusion that sums up the main idea

Introduction
Describes the topic

Body
Supports the main idea with facts and details

Specific details and vivid descriptions keep readers interested.

Hairy Frog

The hairy frog, *Trichobatrachus robustus*, is an unusual species of frogs native to Africa. It is found in west central parts of the continent in subtropical and tropical wet lowlands.

Hairy frogs range in color from olive green to milk-chocolate brown. They grow to be about two-and-one-half inches long. Males are bigger than females and weigh on average three ounces. Hairy frogs have heads wider than long, and the protruding part of their faces, or snouts, are short and rounded. Males have hairlike, thin strands of skin on their sides and thighs. This is what gives *Trichobatrachus robustus* the common name "hairy frog." The hairs are filled with blood vessels that scientists believe help the frogs breathe more easily through their skin.

The hairy frog is sometimes called "horror frog" because of its unusual habit of breaking its own bones. When attacked or threatened, it flexes muscles in its toes and breaks its own toe bones. The bones then pop through the frog's toe pads and create sets of long, sharp claws. This helps hairy frogs defend themselves against predators. No one knows for sure

Other Transitions
Still
Unlike
Similar to
Specifically
After that
By comparison
In conclusion
For example

what happens next, but some scientists think the bones might, sooner or later, pull back inside the skin and the wounds heal over.

Forests, rivers, and croplands make up the hairy frogs' natural habitat. They live mostly on land but return to water for breeding. Their eggs are laid on rocks in streams. Tadpoles are strong and have several rows of sharp teeth for help with eating.

Hairy frogs are meat-eaters. They feed on bugs, including grasshoppers, beetles, and spiders, and even slugs. Most likely, the worst enemy of the hairy frog is humankind. In Cameroon, hairy frogs are hunted for their meat, roasted, and eaten.

Conclusion
Sums up the main topic

This species of frog, known for its strange bone-breaking habit, is a threatened species. As forests are cut down, hairy frogs are losing part of their natural habitat. But for now, hairy frogs are alive and well.

Note how the author of this piece:

- Used vivid words and descriptions.

  . . . from olive green to milk-chocolate brown.

  . . . the protruding part of their faces, or snouts, are short and rounded.

  The bones then pop through the frog's toe pads...

- Organized the information in a way that is clear and easy to understand.

Interview

One way to find information for a news story or research report is to conduct an **interview**.

Parts of an Interview

- The subject's name
- A list of questions for someone knowledgeable
- Questions that ask *who*, *what*, *when*, *where*, *why*, and *how*
- Notes or answers to the questions
- An ending that thanks the subject

The subject's name →

Simon Levy, Winner of the Video Game Showdown

Q: Hi, Simon. Tell me a little bit about yourself.

A: Well, I'm Simon Levy. I'm eleven years old. I'm in the fifth grade at Bowman Elementary School.

Q: What did you just win?

A: I won the Video Game Showdown. It's a gaming contest held downtown. The grand prize was a one-month free pass to Arcadia.

Questions asking the 5Ws and H → Q: Whom did you play against?

A: There were fifty-four players in the contest. They were a mix of kids from ages eight to twelve. My friend Alisha was in the contest as well.

Q: What games did you play?

A: Oh, lots of games. I got lucky in the last round, though. Star Quest was selected for the final. That's my best game.

Q: When did you first start playing?

A: I started playing video games when I was four.

Answers
that show
exactly what
the interview
subject said

Q: Where was the contest held?

A: It was at an arcade downtown called Arcadia. The owner is Mr. Jackson. He also owns that video rental store on Oak Street. I really like Arcadia. They have many kinds of games there, and they put in new games all the time. Plus Mr. Jackson lets the kids have as much popcorn as they want.

Q: Why do you think you won?

A: I play a lot. Well, not too much. My mom makes me stop to do homework and stuff. Also, my older brother Danny coached me.

Q: Did you know any of your competitors?

A: Yeah, my best friend Alisha played, too. She was the runner-up. She's really great. I was worried she would beat me, but I won in the end.

An ending
in which the
interviewer
thanks the
subject

Q: Thank you for talking to me, Simon. Good luck in the contest next year!

A: Thanks for interviewing me!

Note how the author of this piece:

• Asked several kinds of questions to get the interview subject talking.

Other questions she could have asked:

What is your favorite video game?
Where did you learn to play?
How did it feel to win the contest?

• Asked "why" and "how" questions that encouraged Simon to give more information.

Why do you think you won?

Business Letter

A **business letter** is a letter that is written to someone the writer does not know well. It is more formal than a friendly letter. People often write business letters when they want to request something.

Parts of a Business Letter

- A heading, an inside address, and a salutation that includes the recipient's title
- An opening sentence that makes the purpose of the letter clear
- Supporting sentences that add details
- A polite closing and signature

The heading gives the writer's address and the date

1734 North Rd.
Pompano Beach, FL 33093
March 16, 2012

The inside address tells to whom the letter is being sent

Ms. Jennifer McCarthy
Florida Office of Outdoor Recreation
26 State St.
Tallahassee, FL 32395

The salutation uses titles such as *Mr.* or *Ms.*

Dear Ms. McCarthy:

Details tell how the letter's recipient can best help the writer

I would like some information on boating and canoeing in Florida. My parents and I have gone boating in the ocean and on lakes near our home, but I am wondering where else in our state we could go that would be fun. My family does not own any equipment, so we would need to rent a boat or canoe. I am especially interested in places where we can see birds and other wildlife. For example, is it safe to take a boat through the Everglades? I look forward to hearing from you.

Sincerely,
Paula E. Marshall

Closing and Signature

Science Observation Report

In a **science observation report**, the author uses narrative to describe a series of events.

Parts of a Science Observation Report

- The purpose introduces the activity and explains why it is being performed
- Observations describe what was seen or heard by the author
- The conclusion summarizes the report

Purpose
Explains why the observations are being performed and describes some goals

Birds at the Feeder

Purpose:

Our class set up a bird feeder outside our window. We are going to study animal behavior by watching the birds. We will identify the birds that visit and what they do while at the feeder. We will take notes every 10 minutes for one hour.

Observations:

December 1

8:30am: Three birds are at the feeder. I see one cardinal and two sparrows. The cardinal quickly eats the sunflower seeds.

8:40am: One woodpecker has joined the other birds. It leaves right away. Could not see the type of woodpecker.

8:50am: A male and female cardinal are at the feeder.

9:00am: A squirrel is at the feeder! No birds.

9:10am: The squirrel is gone. Two goldfinches are at the feeder. They seem to be eating all the sunflower seeds.

9:20am: The same woodpecker has returned. It fills its beak with seeds before it leaves quickly.

Conclusion: I learned that many different kinds of birds will use a bird feeder. They eat very fast and are always looking around. I also learned that a squirrel will chase away all the birds that are at the feeder.

Observations
Describes what happened during the observation period

Conclusion
Summarizes the observations

Research Report

In a **research report,** the author draws from several different sources to inform the reader about a subject.

Parts of a Research Report

- An introduction that tells what the report is about
- Body paragraphs with topic sentences that are supported by facts and details about the subject
- A conclusion that reviews the main points of the report

Introduction
Lists the subject and some of the main ideas

The author researched the subject to gather facts and details used in this report.

Citations tell the reader where the author found this information.

Endangered Species: Bald Eagle

The bald eagle is a large bird of prey that lives in North America. It is one of our most beautiful birds and our nation's symbol. Placed on the Endangered Species List in 1967 because there were very few left in the wild, the bald eagle was removed from the Endangered Species List in 2007 (Sibley, 125). This makes it one of the few animals to be removed from the list because its population is recovering. The bald eagle is one great success story of the Endangered Species Act.

Life History

Bald eagles live all across North America, from southern Florida to Alaska. Since they mainly catch and eat fish, bald eagles like to live by rivers, lakes, or other large bodies of water. Their powerful talons also help these birds catch and eat turtles, snakes, and other animals (All About Birds).

Bald eagles make the largest nests of any bird in North America. Some of these nests can be 10 feet high and weigh

Other Transitions
Another
Besides
For instance
For example
Because of
Similar to
However
In the end

Headings tell the reader what each section is about. They help the reader find information quickly.

2,000 pounds! Female bald eagles lay one to three eggs each year (Sibley, 127). Both parents help raise the young chicks once they hatch.

Population Decline and Recovery

About 70 years ago, many bald eagles started to die off. Scientists believe this was due to several reasons. First, it was still legal to hunt bald eagles. At the same time, growing cities ruined much of the birds' habitat. But, according to scientists, the main reason bald eagles were dying was DDT, a chemical that was popular for killing insects (All About Birds). Unfortunately, DDT was also very harmful to the environment. The chemical was thinning the shells of bald eagle eggs, so the chicks would die before they could hatch. Some scientists believe that only about 800 adult bald eagles were alive by 1960 (All About Birds).

The government banned the use of DDT in 1972, and the bald eagle population quickly began to recover. Today, scientists estimate that more than 100,000 bald eagles now live in North America (Sibley, 130).

Conclusion

Conclusion
Reviews some of the main points of the report

The bald eagle is one of the most beautiful animals in the world. It is also a true survivor. The recovery of bald eagle populations in North America is a great success story, an example of how we can save our endangered species.

References

References tell the reader exactly where the author found the facts and details in the report.

Sibley, David Allen. *The Sibley Guide to Birds*. Knopf, New York, NY. 2000.

All About Birds. "Bald Eagle." http://www.---.org/guide/bald_eagle.html. Retrieved 12/5/11.

Graphs, Diagrams, and Charts

Graphs, diagrams, and charts can be helpful in describing data. They can be used to compare things or simply illustrate an idea or concept.

Graphs and Charts
Use these to compare data or show how things change over time.

Line Graphs
This type of graph is used to show how something changes over time.

Pie Charts
Use pie charts to illustrate percentage of a whole.

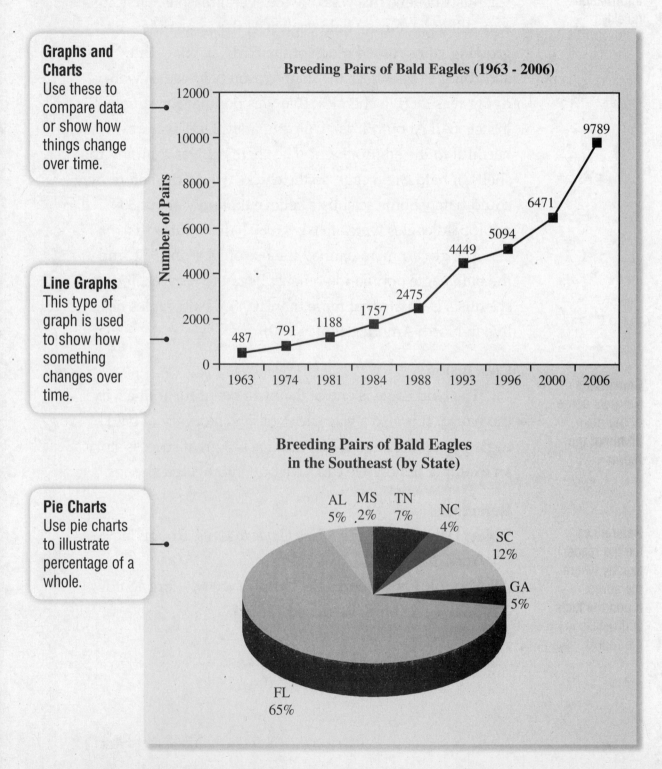

Breeding Pairs of Bald Eagles (1963 - 2006)

Breeding Pairs of Bald Eagles
in the Southeast (by State)

Bar Graphs
These graphs can be used to compare different values.

Titles and Labels
Each graph or chart has a clear title and labels that explain what the data is showing.

Caption and Source
A caption can explain a graph or diagram. A source tells the reader where the information came from.

Diagrams
Use diagrams to demonstrate certain ideas or concepts.

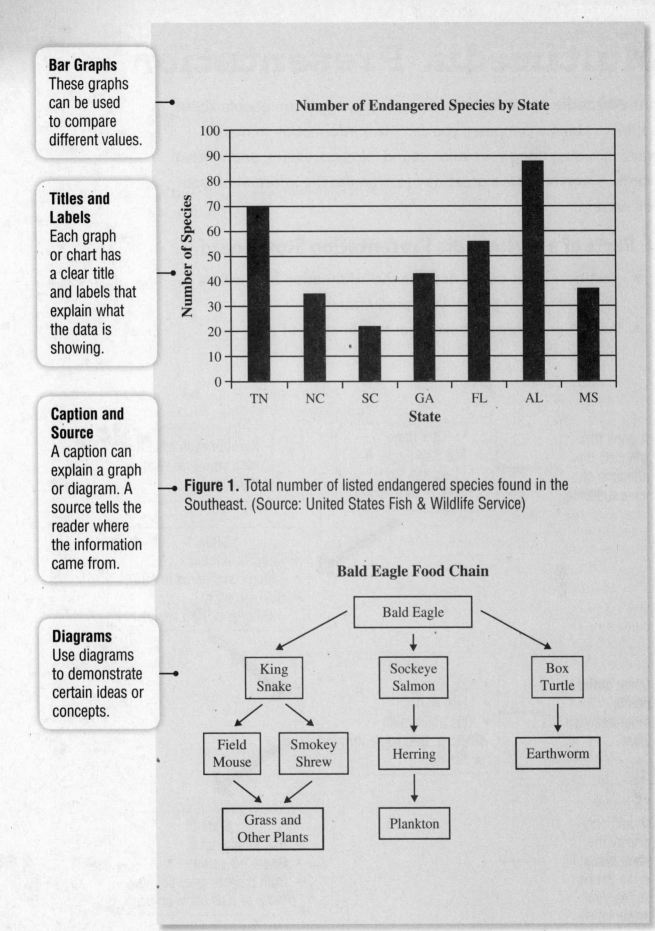

Number of Endangered Species by State

Number of Species (y-axis: 0 to 100)

State (x-axis): TN, NC, SC, GA, FL, AL, MS

Figure 1. Total number of listed endangered species found in the Southeast. (Source: United States Fish & Wildlife Service)

Bald Eagle Food Chain

Bald Eagle
- King Snake
  - Field Mouse → Grass and Other Plants
  - Smokey Shrew → Grass and Other Plants
- Sockeye Salmon
  - Herring
    - Plankton
- Box Turtle
  - Earthworm

Multimedia Presentation

A **multimedia presentation** is a great way to inform people about a subject. Using a computer, you can share information in many ways, including using your voice, sound, pictures, videos, and written words. A storyboard is a great way to organize the information you will present.

Parts of a Multimedia Presentation Storyboard

- Text boxes that briefly describe the information that will be included in each part of your presentation
- Arrows or numbered boxes that tell the story of your presentation

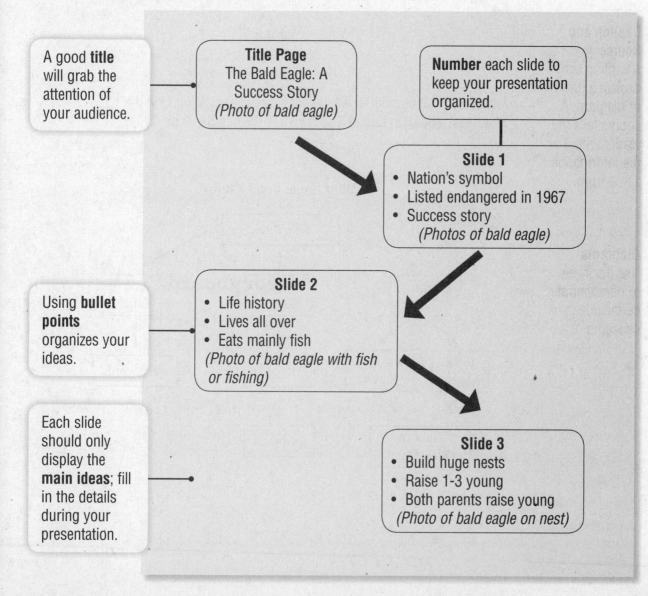

A good **title** will grab the attention of your audience.

Title Page
The Bald Eagle: A Success Story
(Photo of bald eagle)

Number each slide to keep your presentation organized.

Slide 1
- Nation's symbol
- Listed endangered in 1967
- Success story
  (Photos of bald eagle)

Using **bullet points** organizes your ideas.

Slide 2
- Life history
- Lives all over
- Eats mainly fish
(Photo of bald eagle with fish or fishing)

Each slide should only display the **main ideas**; fill in the details during your presentation.

Slide 3
- Build huge nests
- Raise 1-3 young
- Both parents raise young
  (Photo of bald eagle on nest)

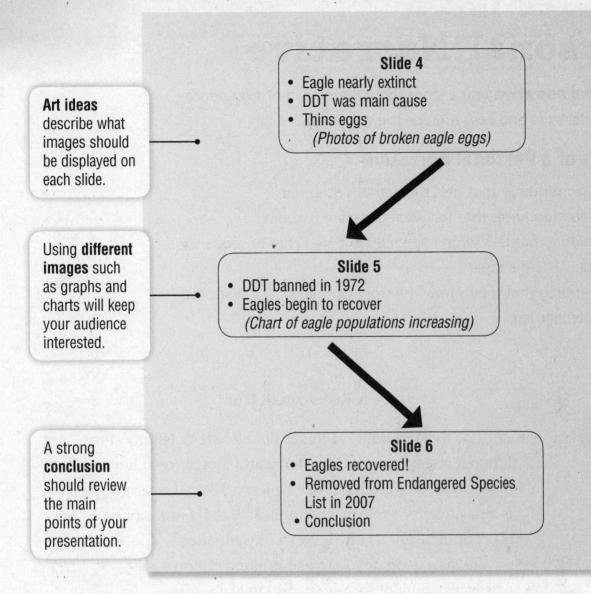

Art ideas describe what images should be displayed on each slide.

Using **different images** such as graphs and charts will keep your audience interested.

A strong **conclusion** should review the main points of your presentation.

Slide 4
- Eagle nearly extinct
- DDT was main cause
- Thins eggs
    (Photos of broken eagle eggs)

Slide 5
- DDT banned in 1972
- Eagles begin to recover
    (Chart of eagle populations increasing)

Slide 6
- Eagles recovered!
- Removed from Endangered Species List in 2007
- Conclusion

Note how the creator of this storyboard:

- Used text boxes to briefly describe what will be included on each slide of the multimedia presentation. The details will be shared with the audience through an oral report.

- Used numbers and arrows to show how the presentation tells a story about the subject. A well-organized presentation will help keep the audience interested in the subject.

Personal Narrative

A **personal narrative** tells a story about an important experience in the writer's life and how it made the writer feel.

✏ Parts of a Personal Narrative

- A lead sentence that gets the reader's attention
- Several sentences that tell what the story is about
- A middle that tells what happened in time order or sequence
- Details and dialogue
- An ending that shows how the story worked out or what the writer learned

Beginning
Interesting first sentence

Middle
Tells story in time order

Vivid details and personal thoughts and feelings

A Risky Fossil Hunt

If it wasn't for luck, I might not be here to tell my story. It happened when my Uncle Jerry and I went fossil hunting in the Robledo Mountains. Uncle Jerry is very brave, and he is a risk taker. Or maybe I should say that he was a risk taker until he got us into a very risky situation.

It was a good day for fossil hunting. The weather was warm, but not too warm, and the sun was shining, making it easy to see fossils in the rocks. First, Uncle Jerry drove us in his Jeep up the rocky trails. Then we hiked to a new spot. He said that no man except him had ever been there before and that I would be the only other person who knew where it was.

Uncle Jerry had a chisel and hammer in his knapsack and enough water and granola bars for us both. He let me carry the pry bar. After hiking a while, we climbed up a steep, rocky hill. Finally, we reached the top, and I felt happy to start looking for fossils.

Other Transitions
First
Then
After hiking a while
Finally
Suddenly
Before
Now

Suddenly, I heard a noise coming from a creosote bush about ten feet away. *Snort-snort-grunt.* "Uncle Jerry," I asked, "what's that sound?"

Before he could answer, out scampered a baby javelina. If you don't know what that is, it's a wild pig. The baby was so cute with its fat, hairy body, long legs, and piggy snout.

Dialogue helps make the story interesting.

"Freeze!" said Uncle Jerry. "Don't move."

I stood still. It felt like time and everything else froze. I sensed something behind me, and then I heard a *snort-snort-grunt* much louder than the baby's.

"Easy. Easy," Uncle Jerry whispered. "Don't move. Don't even look at the baby. Its mother is about twenty feet behind you, and she's real mad."

Oh great, I thought. We're stuck between a killer pig and its baby, and no one knows where we are. My heart pounded hard. Then I felt a whoosh of air as the baby javelina rushed past my leg. The mother followed. I almost screamed, but I didn't. *Snort-snort-grunt. Snort-snort-grunt.* Their cries disappeared into the distance.

"Close call," said Uncle Jerry.

Ending
Tells what the writer learned

I breathed a sigh of relief. Though the rocky hill that Uncle Jerry had found was a great place for fossil hunting, it was also filled with cute but wild animals. That day, I learned how important it is to stay calm in an emergency. I also learned that some risks are not always worth taking.

Biography

A **biography** is a true story that describes a person, not only how he or she looks, but also his or her personality. A well-written biography helps readers to "see" the person and know what he or she is like.

Parts of a Biography

- An interesting beginning paragraph that gets readers' attention and introduces the person
- Several paragraphs that describe the person
- An ending paragraph with a few final thoughts

Beginning
First sentence gets readers' attention

Other sentences introduce the person

Middle
Shows readers what the person is like

My Brother Ben

Most kids want to do something important when they grow up. Ben, my big brother, always wanted to help people. Now, he is a paramedic at the fire station, and his job is saving lives. I think Ben's life is just as exciting as the lives of paramedics you see in stories on TV.

The first thing you notice about Ben is that he is always in a hurry. I guess that is because he has to hurry in his job. When a code sounds in the firehouse, Ben yells to his partner, "Hey! Let's roll." Then he throws on his blue paramedic jacket with the round fire department patch on its shoulder, and he runs to the shiny, red rescue truck. Before you can count to ten, Ben is belted into the driver's seat wearing his mirrored sunglasses, and off they go, working the lights and siren as they race down the street.

Ben is a great storyteller. Whenever he is home for dinner, he tells us about the lives he has saved. Sometimes,

Describing words
Blue
Round
Shiny
Mirrored
Short, red hair
Playful grin
Tall
Happy

The writer adds information about Ben's looks: short red hair, playful grin

he exaggerates a little. One night he told me, "Dude, you should have seen me work on this guy who fell off a ladder and broke his leg in a hundred places." I always know when Ben is stretching the truth because he runs his fingers through his short, red hair. Sometimes his stories are kind of gross. He gets a playful grin on his face when he tells one of those stories because he knows that our mom is going to say, "Ben, not at the dinner table!"

What I like best about Ben is that he loves to help people. Even when he isn't working, he helps the people in our neighborhood. My brother is a pretty tall guy, so he is great at things like painting houses and cleaning out gutters.

Ending
Wraps things up with interesting final thoughts

Old people like him, and kids do, too. He always has time to teach my friends and me a few things about basketball or let us help when he's painting or building something.

The fire department is lucky to have a happy guy like Ben working for them. Not only is he someone everybody likes, but he is also a hero who saves lives. In addition to all that, Ben is an awesome brother.

Note how the author of this piece:

- Used words that show instead of tell. Descriptive words help readers to "see" the person.

  Then he throws on his blue paramedic jacket with the round fire department patch on its shoulder, and he runs to the shiny, red rescue truck.

- Added dialogue to help readers imagine what the person sounds like.

  "Dude, you should have seen me work on this guy who fell off a ladder and broke his leg in a hundred places."

Fictional Narrative

A **fictional narrative** is a short story about made-up characters who need to solve some sort of problem or conflict.

Parts of a Fictional Narrative

- A beginning that introduces the characters, setting, and problem
- A middle that builds excitement as characters try to solve the problem
- An ending that shows how the problem was solved

Stuck in a Maze

Beginning
Introduces the characters, setting, and problem

"Do you know where we are?" Ethan asked his buddy Max as they stood among the tall rows of corn.

"In a corn maze?" Max said. "And lost," he added. "It's going to be dark out soon, and I don't have a clue how to get out of here."

The boys had biked to the pumpkin farm down the road from where they lived. When they got there, they decided to walk through the corn maze. They had been lost for more than an hour, and no one else was around.

Setting Words
In a corn maze
Pumpkin farm
Down the road from where they lived
Going to be dark out soon

"My mom and dad will worry if I'm not home before dark," said Ethan.

Middle
Shows characters trying to solve the problem

"Mine too," answered Max. "It would be better if we could find our way out of here than if they have to come looking for us."

Ethan and Max thought for a while. Then Ethan said, "Hey, the sun sets in the west."

"Yeah," said Max. "So what?"

"We went in the corn maze from the east," said Ethan.

He pointed to his right. "If the sun is setting that way, then east is this way." He pointed to his left. "Let's go!"

So Ethan and Max hurried east, but with all the twists and turns in the maze, they lost track of where they were going. By now, the sun had disappeared behind the tall cornstalks.

This is the climax, or the high point of the story.

"I think we're lost again," said Max. "Maybe we should yell for help. This is getting spooky."

Ethan didn't like the idea of asking for help. Not yet, at least. Then he heard something rustling nearby in the corn. "What's that?" he whispered as he felt a chill run up his spine.

Out from the corn came a chubby brown and white dog.

Dialogue makes the characters seem real and helps move the story along.

"I remember seeing this dog at the pumpkin farm," said Max. "I think it lives there." A big smile spread across Max's face. "I have an idea," he said. "Go home, boy!" When he said it, the dog started barking and running through the maze. "Follow him!" Max cried.

Max and Ethan had to run really fast to keep up with the dog. First, a left turn and a right turn. Next another right. Then a left. Finally, they ran out of the maze and into the wide-open pumpkin field. The dog barked and romped around them.

Ending
Shows how the characters solved the conflict

"Whew," said Ethan, huffing and puffing from running so fast. "I thought we were really lost."

"Me, too," said Max. "And I confess that I was scared."

"So was I, until that dog came along," Ethan agreed. "I won't tell anyone we were lost if you won't." He smiled.

"It'll be our secret," said Max. "Shake on it."

The boys shook hands and headed home.

Science Fiction Story

A **science fiction story** is a made-up story set in another time or place, usually the future.

Parts of a Science Fiction Story

- A beginning that introduces the characters, setting, and problem
- A middle that tells what happened in another time or place and includes some sort of science or technology
- An ending that shows how the problem was solved

Poof! 3012

Beginning
Introduces the characters, setting, and problem

It all started when my five-year-old brother made make-believe milkshakes in our kitchen. While I pretended to drink one, my brother said, "I am the wizard, and poof, you are gone." And suddenly, poof, I was gone! Well, I wasn't really gone. I was invisible and standing in our kitchen in the year 3012. The date flashed on a high-tech calendar on the kitchen wall.

Other Transitions
First
Next
After that
During
After a while
Later
Last

Our kitchen looked like something from Mars. Red lights flashed. Things whirled and beeped. I had an odd feeling that all the strange gadgets were watching me. I really wanted to go home. But wait. I was home. Well, sort of.

Middle
Tells what happened and includes science, technology, and sometimes beings from another world

Just then, the back door opened. A lady and a boy walked in. Their faces were silver, green, and ugly.

"Aliens!" I gasped, and I hid under the kitchen table. I forgot that I was invisible. The alien mom pushed a button on the wall. A robot popped out of a cabinet.

"Groceries," said the mom. Then the robot scooted

outside and came back with three silver bags filled with food. It unpacked them and put the cold foods into a tall, black box in the kitchen. When the robot opened the box, the inside glowed an eerie purple, and the box said, "Milk, cheese, butter. You forgot the eggs again."

This paragraph shows the climax, or the high point of the story.

Meanwhile, the alien boy sat down on the kitchen floor next to the table where I was hiding. Was it my imagination, or was he staring at me? Could he see me? I didn't know whether to scream or cry. I wanted to be back in my old familiar kitchen. I wanted my old mom and my old little brother.

The alien boy looked at me with cold, black eyes. Wait. He had a stick in his hand. It glowed bright, sparkly green. He pointed it at me. Oh, no! He did see me. "I am the wizard," he said. "And poof, you are gone."

Ending
Tells how the problem or conflict worked out

I blinked and then opened my eyes. I was back in our present-day kitchen still pretending to drink my brother's fake milkshake. "Alex," I said to him. "Can you see me?"

My brother gave me a curious look. "Of course, I can see you," he said. "What is your problem?"

Note how the author of this piece:

- Includes futuristic objects and people in her story.

  The date flashed on a high-tech calendar on the kitchen wall.

  Their faces were silver, green, and ugly.

  . . . the inside glowed an eerie purple, and the box said, "Milk, cheese, butter. You forgot the eggs again."

- Tells how the main character feels.

  I had an odd feeling that all the strange gadgets were watching me.

  I didn't know whether to scream or cry.

Play

A **play** is a story told through dialogue and action. The writer makes up the conversations and actions for characters. Then real people read and act out the characters' parts.

Parts of a Play

- A beginning, middle, and ending
- Characters who have to solve a problem or conflict
- A plot, or series of events, that make up the story

Who Stole the Blueberries?

List of characters and a brief description of each →

Characters:

JAKE, 11 years old

MARI, his teen-aged sister

MOM, their mother

CHECKERS, the family dog

The place where the play begins →

Setting: The family's kitchen at breakfast

ACT 1

Words inside ( ) help actors know how to act and say their parts

Beginning Introduces the problem or conflict →

(*Jake and Mari sit at the kitchen table eating cereal. A cereal box is on the table. Mari gets up, opens the refrigerator, and looks inside.*)

MARI: Hey, where are all the blueberries?

JAKE: (*not interested, picks up the cereal box and starts reading the back of it*) How should I know?

Middle Shows how characters try to solve the problem or conflict →

MARI: (*shuts the refrigerator door, clearly upset with her younger brother*) You know what happened to them, don't you? I know you do, because you love blueberries! (*She stands with her hands on her hips.*)

JAKE: (*looks at her, irritated*) I didn't eat the stupid blueberries. Maybe Freddie ate them.

MARI: (*sits down at the table*) Don't blame Freddie. At sixteen months he can barely walk, let alone open the fridge and steal a plastic bag full of berries.

JAKE: (*arguing*) Don't be so sure. He gets into everything. Go see if he's blue.

MARI: *You* go!

JAKE: No, *you* go!

MARI: (*annoyed, leaves the scene for a little while, then returns to her place at the table*) Freddie is asleep in his swing, and he's not blue. I still think *you* ate the berries.

JAKE: (*Loudly*) I did not! Stop blaming me for something I didn't do.

MOM: (*Enters the scene quickly*) What are you two fighting about?

MARI: Jake ate all the blueberries, and I wanted some on my cereal.

JAKE: I'm telling the truth, Mom. I didn't eat her dumb berries.

MOM: I took the bag of berries out of the fridge about a half hour ago, and I put it on the counter. (*She looks at Jake suspiciously.*) Jake, are you *sure* you didn't eat the berries?

JAKE: (*shakes his head and sighs*)

(*Checkers romps into the kitchen. He runs in circles, chasing his tail. Jake sees that the dog's face is stained blue.*)

JAKE: Hey, look at Checkers. *He* ate the blueberries.

MARI: (*looks guiltily at Jake*) I'm sorry for blaming you, I guess.

MOM: (*speaking to Checkers*) What should we do with our little blue dog?

JAKE: (*with a playful smile*) Cheer him up!

(*Mom and Mari groan.*)

Use *italics* when you want actors to emphasize a word

Ending Shows how the problem or conflict is solved

Opinion Essay

An **opinion essay** explains the writer's personal view about a topic. It also includes reasons to support the writer's view.

Parts of an Opinion Essay

- An introduction that clearly states the writer's opinion
- A body that supports the opinion with reasons
- A conclusion that summarizes the opinion

Introduction
Clearly states the opinion

Body
Has paragraphs that state facts and examples to support the opinion

Transitions
The best reason
Another reason
Also
In conclusion

I Think Zoos Should be Illegal

Many people like zoos, but I think they should be illegal. Wild animals suffer in zoos. They need to live in the wild in their natural environments instead of being locked up in cages and pens.

The best reason that zoos should be illegal is that big animals, like elephants, do poorly in zoos. The life span of elephants in zoos is much less than elephants in the wild. Zoo elephants die because they don't have enough space to move around. They eat a lot, but they don't exercise much. Then they become overweight. Overweight elephants can die from heart attacks, just like overweight people. In the wild, elephants have miles and miles of space to move around, so they burn off their extra fat.

Another reason is that some animals get so bored that they develop a condition called zoochosis. This means they do the same thing over and over. Some examples of zoochosis are when animals bite the bars of their cages, lick a lot, bob their heads, or pace back and forth or in circles. People laugh and think the animals are being funny.

However, these poor animals are losing their minds from being locked up.

Also, imagine how alone you would feel if you came from a very big family and then suddenly you were an only child. Even your parents were gone. That is how some zoo animals must feel. A zoo can be a very lonely place for animals that live in herds in the wild. Think of that one rhinoceros in the zoo, or that one elephant, giraffe, or wolf. Instinct tells these animals that they should be part of a big family. Instead they live by themselves in zoos.

Conclusion
Restates the opinion using different words

In conclusion, I think wild animals need to be where they belong, in the wild in their natural habitats. We could learn so much more about these animals by watching them on web cams or in documentaries. Best of all, wild animals would be happier, healthier, and live longer if zoos were made illegal.

Note how the author of this piece:

- Used facts and examples to support her reasons.

  The life span of elephants in zoos is much less than elephants in the wild.

  Some examples of zoochosis are when animals bite the bars of their cages, lick a lot, bob their heads, or pace back and forth or in circles.

- Used transitions to effectively move from one paragraph to the next. Other transitions she might have used include:

  Another issue, second, last

Persuasive Essay

The purpose of a **persuasive essay** is to convince readers to agree with the writer's opinion and take a certain action.

Parts of a Persuasive Essay

- An introduction that describes the topic and clearly states the writer's opinion
- Several body paragraphs, each offering a specific reason and details to support the opinion
- A conclusion that calls readers to take action

Eat Your Brussels Sprouts

Beginning
Describes the topic and contains the opinion statement

Do you eat Brussels sprouts? Some people hate Brussels sprouts, those vegetables that look like little cabbages. They don't know that Brussels sprouts are healthy and delicious. Everyone should give Brussels sprouts a try.

Body
Has paragraphs that begin with one main reason and include details to support it

First of all, Brussels sprouts do not have to taste bitter. If you toast them in the oven instead of boiling them, they get crispy on the outside and taste sweet and crunchy. You can put shredded cheese on them to make them taste even better. Another way to make Brussels sprouts taste good is to cut them in half and stir-fry them with other kinds of vegetables. Add some pieces of chicken and a few cashews to your stir-fry, and you will love the taste. Everyone who hates Brussels sprouts should try them prepared in different ways.

Other Transitions
For instance
Of course
For example
As a result
To begin with
In addition

Also, Brussels sprouts are good for you. In 2010, a government study showed that two-thirds of Americans were overweight. Brussels sprouts are low in fat and calories. There are only 50 calories in a whole cup.

Plus, they are loaded with fiber and Vitamin A, which is good for your eyes, and Vitamin C, which prevents colds. People who hate Brussels sprouts have to agree that Brussels sprouts are good for their health.

Usually, the most important reason comes last.

Most important, Brussels sprouts are so good for you that they are known as a superfood. Scientists are studying them to learn how they might help fight certain diseases. Some scientists believe that sulforaphane, a chemical found in Brussels sprouts, might help prevent cancer. Best of all, they say that people should not boil Brussels sprouts because boiling makes sulforaphane less powerful. Brussels sprouts haters should like this news because boiled Brussels sprouts don't taste very good.

Conclusion Summarizes the opinion and calls readers to take action

Brussels sprouts can be tasty if you prepare them the right way. They are excellent for your health. And you have to admit that, as far as vegetables go, these little cabbages are really cute. So, even if you are a Brussels sprouts hater, you should agree to give them another try.

Note how the author of this piece:

- Included a clear opinion statement in the first paragraph.

  Everyone should give Brussels sprouts a try.

- Added facts to support his opinion.

  In 2010, a government study showed that two-thirds of Americans were overweight.

- Ended by calling readers to action.

  So, even if you are a Brussels sprouts hater, you should agree to give them another try.

Response to a Play

When writing a **response to a play**, the writer can choose to review the play as a whole or to write about a part of it: theme, plot, a favorite character, dialogue, setting, or costumes.

Parts of a Response to a Play

- An introduction that gives a brief overview of the play's plot
- A body that reviews the entire play or one specific element
- A conclusion that includes the writer's feelings about the play or the chosen part of the play

Introduction
Includes a brief description of the play's plot

Organization
First ghost
Second ghost
Last ghost

Body
Reviews the entire play or one of its elements

Vivid details help readers imagine the character.

Response to "A Christmas Carol"

Last weekend, my family and I attended the high school's play, "A Christmas Carol," by Charles Dickens. The play showed how a mean, old man named Ebenezer Scrooge became just as kind as he once was selfish.

In the play, three ghosts visit Ebenezer Scrooge in his bedroom at separate times in the night. The ghosts were my favorite characters in the play. Each one was different.

A short kid played the first ghost, the Ghost of Christmas Past. I couldn't tell if it was a boy or girl, or if the ghost was supposed to be a kid or a grown-up. I think not knowing made the character more interesting. It made me wonder about who the ghost was and where it came from. This ghost was gentle and quiet. It led mean, old selfish Ebenezer Scrooge, who hated Christmas, back into his past. It showed him how he had lived from childhood to the present.

The Ghost of Christmas Present, the second ghost, was a big, tall actor dressed in a crown and a kingly, green robe. He had a big, booming voice that was loud and jolly. When he first appeared on stage, he stood by a banquet table loaded with delicious holiday foods. You could hear the audience ooh and ahh because he looked so royal. This ghost showed Scrooge how other people where he lived celebrated and enjoyed Christmas. I liked him because he was larger than life in both his size and his personality.

Comparisons are used to help readers imagine the characters.

The last ghost, The Ghost of Christmas Future, belonged more in a Halloween play than one about Christmas. This ghost was very scary. It was tall and wore a black, hooded robe. Unlike the other ghosts, it never showed its face, and it didn't speak. The stage lighting was blue and eerie, which made the ghost even spookier. The ghost showed Ebenezer the future and how people wouldn't like him because he was so mean. It even took Scrooge to a graveyard and showed him a tombstone with his name on it!

Conclusion Wraps things up and shows how the writer felt

The three ghosts were my favorite characters because they helped Scrooge turn his life around. When he saw himself as a kid and then saw how he had become mean and selfish, Scrooge wanted to be better. I liked it that he changed. Best of all, he became a caring, helpful man.

Note how the author of this piece:

- Wrote only about one element of the play: her favorite characters, the ghosts.

  Other elements she could have written about include:

  the setting, where the play takes place

  the dialogue and how characters' words came to life on the stage

- Concluded with an explanation of her feelings about the characters.

  The three ghosts were my favorite characters because they helped Scrooge turn his life around.

Response to Poetry

When responding to a **poem**, the writer may write about the kind of poem, the way the poet uses words, and the meaning of the poem or how it made the writer feel.

Parts of a Response to a Poem

- The introduction names the poem and its author and describes the poem's form
- The body describes the special way the poet used words
- The conclusion tells what the poem means or how the writer felt about it

Introduction
Names the poem and poet and describes the poem's form

Body
Explains the special way the poet used words

"Line Up for Yesterday": A Response

The poem "Line Up for Yesterday: An ABC of Baseball Immortals" was written by the poet Ogden Nash. It is a poem based on letters of the alphabet. This poem is different from other ABC poems that have one word or one line of words for each alphabet letter. Instead, Ogden Nash wrote a four-line rhyming poem for each letter of the alphabet.

First, Mr. Nash chose a famous baseball player's name for each ABC. The player's last name matches the alphabet letter, like "A" for Grover Cleveland Alexander, "B" for Roger Bresnahan, and "C" for Ty Cobb. Then, he wrote a four-line rhyme about each player. His poem was special because it was actually many short poems that made up one long poem.

Some of the mini-poems tell why a player was great or how he played the game. Others tell how Ogden Nash felt about the player. He even put himself in the poem for the letter "I". He described himself as "an incurable fan."

The first line of each mini-poem begins with an alphabet letter and a baseball player's name, A is for Alex, B

Each middle
paragraph
tells one thing
about the poem
and backs it
up with facts,
examples, or
details.

is for Bresnahan, C is for Cobb. The second and fourth lines always end in a rhyme, like corn-born, love-glove, and truth-Ruth.

In just a few words, Mr. Nash shows what some of the players looked like. He describes things like Johnny Evers's jaw, a pitcher throwing to Roger Hornsby, and Mel Ott's restless right foot.

Conclusion
Tells how the
writer felt about
the poem, or
what the poem
means

As a baseball fan, I loved this poem by Ogden Nash. Some of his rhymes made me laugh. Many of them taught me things that I didn't know about these old-time baseball players. I especially liked how his words helped me to imagine these players in action.

Note how the author of this piece:

- Gave specific examples to explain how the poet uses words.

  The player's last name matches the alphabet letter, like "A" for Grover Cleveland Alexander, "B" for Roger Bresnahan, and "C" for Ty Cobb.

- Ended the response by telling how he feels about Ogden Nash's poem.

  Other ways he could have ended the response are to tell what he thinks the poem means, or explain why he thinks Ogden Nash wrote it:

  Ogden Nash's poem means that baseball has had many great players.

  I think Ogden Nash wrote this poem because he really loved baseball.

Author Response

An **author response** is an essay about the writings of one specific author. The writer tells about the author's works and also includes his or her own feelings.

✏ Parts of an Author Response

- An introduction that describes the author
- A body that tells why the writer likes the author's works
- A conclusion that sums up the writer's opinion of the author

Introduction
Describes the author

Roald Dahl

Roald Dahl is one of my favorite authors. His first name is kind of strange. It is Roald, not Ronald. His books are a little strange, too, and that is why I like them. My favorites are <u>Matilda</u> and <u>Charlie and the Chocolate Factory</u>.

One thing I like about Roald Dahl is the way he names his characters. The names he chooses make readers laugh. For example, Matilda's last name is Wormwood. She went to a school called Crunchem Hall. Two teachers there are named Miss Honey and Miss Trunchbull, and their names fit their personalities.

Body
Gives reasons why the writer likes the author and includes details and examples

In <u>Charlie and the Chocolate Factory,</u> you will find Charlie Bucket, Augustus Gloop, Willy Wonka, and a silly group of little men called Oompa-Loopas. Almost all of the characters in Roald Dahl's books have amusing names.

Another thing I like about Roald Dahl is that his writing includes lots of descriptions that help readers imagine what the settings and characters look like. In <u>Charlie and the Chocolate Factory</u>, Roald Dahl describes a chocolate-mixing room, but it looks

Other Transitions
The first
The next
The last
Finally
Also
In addition to
Last of all

like a garden. Everything there is made of candy, and he even put a chocolate lake into the scene. In <u>Matilda</u>, he makes Matilda's super powers believable. You can imagine her staring hard at a glass of water and making it tip over or making a piece of chalk write on the blackboard just by looking at it.

My favorite thing about Roald Dahl's writing is that it can be scary. Some kids don't like his books because of that, but I do. You never know what is going to happen. Maybe an ordinary thing will become weird, like a peach growing as big as a house. A giant might show up and poke his finger through the window, or maybe a shark will come out of nowhere and attack. You never know with Roald Dahl.

Conclusion
Sums up the writer's feelings about the author

Roald Dahl died a while ago. I wish that he were still here to write more stories, but I will never get tired of his books. Some of them I have read more than once. In my opinion, Roald Dahl is one of the greatest authors who ever lived.

Note how the writer of this piece:

- Included several strong reasons why he likes this author.

  One thing I like about Roald Dahl is the way he names his characters.

  Another thing I like about Roald Dahl is that his writing includes lots of descriptions ...

  My favorite thing about Roald Dahl's writing is that it can be scary.

- Organized his reasons, putting the most important one last.

Book Review

A **book review** tells what a book is about without giving away the ending. It also explains the writer's feelings about the book.

Parts of a Book Review

- An introduction that names the book
- A body that tells what the book is about and explains its theme or message
- A conclusion that reveals how the writer felt about the book

Introduction
Names the book

Body
Tells what the story is about without giving away the ending

The Light Princess

The Light Princess is a fairy tale by George MacDonald. It is a very old story, written in 1864. If you haven't read it, then you should because it is fun to read. It is a fairy tale for kids of all ages.

A king and queen want a child very much, and after a while, they have a baby girl. The problems begin at the baby's christening with the king's evil sister, who is a witch. She is really mad that the king didn't invite her to the christening, so she shows up anyway. The wicked woman puts a curse on the baby, taking away her sense of gravity. This means that the Light Princess floats around like a balloon all the time. Whenever she floats up to the ceiling, someone has to pull her down. Sometimes, the wind carries her away.

Along with her gravity problem, the princess giggles all the time. She can't take anything seriously, and she can't cry. Her parents want the floating and giggling to stop, but everything they try fails. Finally, the princess finds one special place where she won't float around, and then she meets a prince. Will he be able to break the curse?

Body
Tells about the book's theme or message

The Light Princess is a funny and sometimes adventurous story that teaches a lesson. Like that famous quote says, "If at first you don't succeed try, try again." Everyone keeps trying to give back to the princess her sense of gravity. Will they succeed, and if so, how will they do it?

Conclusion
Tells what the writer liked about the book

I like The Light Princess because the characters and the plot are so funny. The story exists as a picture book, but I read the chapter book that has no pictures. I liked doing that because it let me imagine the princess floating and giggling and irritating everyone in the kingdom. I also enjoyed the characters' names. The king's evil sister is Princess Makemnoit and the two wise men in the story are named Hum-Drum and Kopy-Keck. Most of all, I liked the way the story ends. When you read it, I know you will, too.

Note how the author of this piece:

- Didn't give away the story's ending

  Finally, the princess finds one special place where she won't float around, and then she meets a prince. Will he be able to break the curse?

- Encouraged her readers to read the book

  Most of all, I liked the way the story ends. When you read it, I know you will, too.

Persuasive Speech

A **persuasive speech** is a lot like a persuasive essay. It has the same parts, but it is spoken aloud. It is written for a very specific audience and uses language that will appeal to that group.

Parts of a Persuasive Speech

- An introduction that catches the listeners' attention and includes an opinion statement
- A body with several strong reasons that support the opinion
- A conclusion that restates the opinion and calls listeners to action

Introduction
Gets the listeners' interest and includes a clear opinion statement

Body
States facts, examples, and details to support the opinion

Each paragraph is about one supporting reason.

Cats are Smarter Than Dogs

Are you a dog person or a cat person? If you're a dog person, then you've probably taught your dog a trick or two. You might even believe that your dog is smart. Well, I'm here to tell you that cats are smarter than dogs.

First, let's look at the scientific facts. Research shows that kitties have 300 million neurons in the thinking part of their brains. Dogs have only 160 million. Scientists at Tufts University of Veterinary Medicine say that the thinking part of a cat's brain is built like a human brain. It even works like a human's.

You're probably thinking, *But Marcus, my dog is really smart because he obeys me, and he does tricks. You can't teach a cat to obey.* And that's another reason why cats are smarter. A cat does what it wants whenever it wants. It knows perfectly well what you mean when you say, "Don't do that." But a cat will find a way to sneak around and do exactly what you don't want it to do. In other words, a dog does pretty much whatever you

Other Transitions
Secondly
Finally
Next
After that
During
After a while
Meanwhile
Later
Last

The most important reason comes last.

ask because it wants to please you and can't think for itself. But a cat will outsmart you every time.

You still don't believe that cats are smarter than dogs? Then consider the most important proof. When a kitten is just a few weeks old, its mother picks it up by the back of its neck and hauls it to the litter box. By the time you adopt a kitten, it already knows where the box is and how to use it. By comparison, a puppy's mother teaches it nothing about using the bathroom. If you adopt a puppy, you can expect to find some not-so-nice surprises on the floor. And when the dog grows up, it uses the bathroom outside, often bringing dirt inside the house. So, which animal is smarter when it comes to using the bathroom? Cats, for sure.

Conclusion Restates the opinion using different words, summarizes the reasons, and calls the audience to take action

In conclusion, unlike dogs, a cat's brain has more neurons and works like a human's. And unlike dogs, cats are independent thinkers. They do what *they* think is best. Finally, cats know the best way to use the bathroom. Believe it or not, some have even been taught to use the toilet and flush. So, while dogs are cute and a human's best friend, you should agree that cats are smarter than dogs.

Note how the author of this piece:

- Thought about her audience—her classmates—and wrote a speech that they would enjoy.

- Spoke directly to her audience.

  Are you a dog person, or a cat person?

  You're still not convinced that cats are smarter than dogs?

- Used casual language that sounded the way her classmates talk.

  You're probably thinking, But, Marcus, my dog is really smart . . .

  . . . a dog does pretty much whatever you ask . . .

Labels and Captions

A **label** explains what a picture is, and a **caption** adds information to a picture. A label uses one or several words. A caption includes one or more complete sentences.

Labels can be one word

Parallelogram

or several words.

Students of the Month

A label is a word or phrase

They may or may not include a verb.

Running a race

Captions explain an idea shown in a picture.

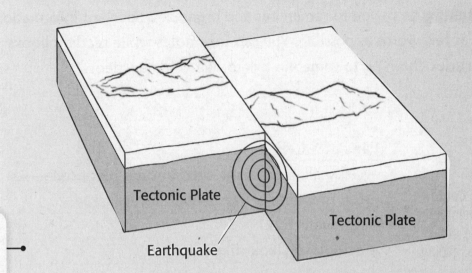

Tectonic Plate

Tectonic Plate

Earthquake

These words label parts of the picture.

This part is the caption.

The earth's crust is made of sheets of rock. A fault forms when a force, like tension or compression, creates stress and causes a break in the rocks.

A caption uses complete sentences.

Captions can add interesting information to a picture.

This is a caption.

Wild polar bears prefer to eat seals. If they cannot find seals to eat, they will eat other mammals, birds, fish, eggs, certain plants, and berries.

Notetaking Strategies

Notetaking helps you to remember and organize important information using as few words as possible. You can take notes while reading books and articles, listening to someone talk, or watching a video.

Note Cards are helpful for taking notes while reading.

Parts of a Cell

—cell wall: membrane surrounding plant cell

—cell membrane: thin protein layer inside

• cell wall

—cytoplasm: looks like jelly

—nucleus: a cell's control center

—mitochondria: changes food into energy

—vacuoles: stores water, food, and

waste material

(Amazing Cells, by William Parker, p.7)

Each note card includes
One main idea

Supporting details

The source where you found the information

Data Charts are another good way to take notes while reading.

Notetaking Data Chart

Your name and topic Sasha Baker Civil War	Question #1 Why did the Civil War happen?	Question #2 Who was Ulysses S. Grant?	Question #3 Who was Robert E. Lee?
Source #1 Encyclopedia of American History, vol. 3	Answer to question #1 from Source #1 Slavery (pp. 77-79)	Answer to question #2 from Source #1 Union Army Leader (p. 85)	Answer to question #3 from Source #1 Confederate Army Leader (p.86)
Source #2 The Civil War, by Lynn Miller	Answer to question #1 from Source #2 States vs. Federal rights	Answer to question #2 from Source #2 Excellent military skills (p. 10)	Answer to question #3 from Source #2 Fierce fighter (p. 11)

Additional columns and rows can be added to include more questions.

A data chart includes

Your name and the main topic

5W&H questions you want to answer about your topic

A brief answer to each question

The source where you found the information

Good notetaking requires practice. When reading and listening, make sure that you understand the information so your notes will be correct. When listening, stay focused so you hear everything the speaker says. The more you practice notetaking, the easier it will become.

Build Your Notetaking Skills

- Pay attention to what you read, hear, or see.

- When listening, write quickly but neatly enough so you can read it later.

- Write down only what is necessary: main ideas and important details. No need to make full sentences.

- Use your own words. Don't copy information word-for-word from articles and books unless you plan to cite the words as a quote in your writing.

- Summarize big pieces of information.

- Draw pictures if they will help you to remember something.

- Organize your information clearly using numbers or transitions like *first, second, third*.

- Be accurate when writing down your sources. Use the title, author's name, and the page number(s) where you found the information.

- Read over your notes right away. Fix anything that is unclear or hard to read.

- Put a star next to main ideas, or highlight them with a marker.

Journal Entry

When you write a **journal entry**, you write in your notebook about anything you want, such as things you have learned or things that have happened to you.

Parts of a Journal Entry

- The date of the entry
- A beginning that introduces the topic
- A middle that includes details and your thoughts and feelings
- An ending thought

November 14

Beginning
Tells what the entry is about

People talk a lot about bullying. We've had assemblies about it at school. There are commercials about it on TV. My friends and I haven't been bullied, and we don't bully other kids. So, to be honest, I didn't think much about it. But today all of that changed.

There's a new girl in the other fifth grade class. Her name is Olga Pedraza. I don't know her very well. I guess I don't know much about any of the kids in the other fifth grade room. I mostly hang out with friends from my class.

Middle
Tells what happened and includes the writer's thoughts and feelings

Well, today in the lunchroom I saw Olga sitting alone. I probably wouldn't have noticed her except that I was hanging out by myself waiting for my best friend, Sophie. Anyhow, Olga was sitting at a table by herself drinking milk when Anthony Bain, from my class, came along with a couple of other guys. He bumped Olga's shoulder really hard, on purpose. She spilled milk all over herself. Then he called her a name and laughed.

I couldn't believe what I saw! Anthony always seems so nice when he's with my friends and me.

Dialogue makes the people and situation more real.

I wanted to walk up to him and say, "Hey, what do you think you're doing?" but I chickened out.

I did what I thought was the next best thing. I asked Olga if I could sit with her. She looked surprised and sort of scared. Then she said, "Sure." And when Sophie came, she joined us.

Olga turned out to be really nice. She and her family just moved here from Mexico City, Mexico. She told us that there are pyramids not far from where she lived. They are called the Pyramid of the Sun and the Pyramid of the Moon. I would like to see them someday. Sophie said that she would, too.

By the time lunch was over, we were friends with Olga. I can't wait to hang out with her more and meet her family.

Ending Shows how the situation wrapped up and includes a final thought

Tomorrow, I plan to do something brave. I'm going to have a talk with Anthony Bain about bullying. Who knows, maybe when I get done with him, he'll want to be friends with Olga, too.

Note how the author of this piece:

- Used informal word choice to tell what happened.

  I mostly hang out with friends from my class.

  . . . I chickened out.

- Wrote about a meaningful experience.

  Other topics she could have written about include

  An event or concert she went to

  A favorite thing or hobby

  Something she learned about in school

  Something that happened to her

Index